THE NOBLE SPUD

The Noble Spud

Judy Wells and Rick Johnson

 PENGUIN BOOKS

Penguin Books Canada Ltd., 2801 John Street, Markham,
Ontario, Canada L3R 1B4
Penguin Books Ltd., Harmondsworth, Middlesex, England
Penguin Books, 40 West 23rd Street, New York, New York 10010 U.S.A.
Penguin Books Australia Ltd., Ringwood, Victoria, Australia
Penguin Books (N.Z.) Ltd., Private Bag, Takapuna, Auckland 9,
New Zealand

First published by Penguin Books Canada Ltd., 1985

Canadian Cataloguing in Publication Data

Wells, Judy.
The noble spud

Includes index.
ISBN 0-14-046687-8

1. Cookery (Potatoes).   2. Potatoes.   I. Johnson,
Rick.   II. Title.

TX803.P8W45 1985   641.6'521   C85-098647-8

Drawings by
Christine Oleksyk
Book design by
Catherine Wilson/Sunkisst Graphics
Photography by
Hal Roth Photography
Food stylist
Judy Wells
Manufactured in Canada by
Gagne Printing Ltd.
Typesetting by
Jay Tee Graphics Ltd.

Front cover photograph
Scalloped Potatoes

For Marie Joyce Cecile,
a mother who taught much more than cooking
and touched everything with her love and generosity

A NOTE ON METRICATION

The recipes in this book are given in both imperial and metric measures. The metric measurements are not exact conversions of the imperial measurements but have been rounded off to standard metric units. The basic proportion of ingredients remains consistent.

ACKNOWLEDGEMENT

With grateful thanks to Mary Adachi, our editor, for her sensitive prodding, tact and good humour.

Contents

Introduction

About 8,000 years ago, on the hillsides of Peru grew the ancestor of our potato. Archeologists, foraging in the kitchen middens and fossilized garbage dumps high in the Andes Mountains, have found remnants of potatoes.

The journey of the potato from ancient Peru to the modern world parallels the history of European discovery and conquest. The Spanish introduced potato plants to various regions of South and North America before taking them home to Spain, around 1539. They also introduced the potato to Ireland during their many forays along the Irish coast.

Throughout its early history in the northern hemisphere, the potato was greatly misunderstood. The word "potato" is a corruption of the South American Indian word "batata," meaning yam — a member of another botanical family altogether. At first it was sought after in the courts of Spain, France and England not as food but as an ornamental plant. Its full, pinnate leaves and delicate flowers were much admired. The well-to-do exchanged bouquets of potato flowers, and fashionable men and women wore the blossoms as boutonnières. In eighteenth-century Russia they were known as "the devil's apples." There, as in other parts of Europe, foods which grew under the ground were regarded with suspicion and associated with both dirt and unchristian behaviour.

While there was grudging belief in some medicinal benefits of the potato — cut potatoes were rubbed on sprains, warts and black eyes — potatoes were suspected of causing everything from flatulence to syphilis. In some parts of Italy it was believed that you could dispose of an enemy by writing his name on a potato. In Ireland the potato was suspected of producing lust and achieved notoriety as a fashionable cure for impotence.

However, in South America the potato was a staple food and a valued crop. The Quechua Indians had a thousand words in their language to describe potatoes. The Incas measured time by how long it took a potato to cook. Anthropologists are still uncovering signs of South American rituals which celebrated or appeased potato gods. It is said that when potato crops failed, the custom was to chop off the noses of several unfortunate Indians. It is interesting to note that the early South American potato was barely larger than an unshelled peanut.

Today the world-wide annual production of potatoes is estimated at 300 million tons (136 million tonnes), but it took nearly three hundred years for the potato to find acceptance as food in Europe and North America.

Until the early seventeenth century, the staple food in the British Isles was grain. This dependence on grain was altered during the uprisings in Ireland when English soldiers attempted to quell the rebellion by destroying the crops. The Irish discovered that potatoes, grown underground, were less likely to be destroyed than grain. The Irish tenant farmers with only tiny plots of poor land on which to grow food for their own families also found the potato to be an ideal crop because it produced a higher yield than grains.

The potato was easy to cultivate. The farmer laid a row of seed potatoes on the ground, dug a trench alongside and covered them with soil. When the shoots appeared, he merely piled on more soil. To the English this method was laughably primitive, but it suited the stoney and boggy Irish land. The trenches provided good drainage on the bogs, and plots could be extended onto mountain slopes which would not take a plough. In fact, all the farmer needed was a spade. It is said that the word ''spud'' is derived from ''spade.''

Although the English first regarded the potato with scorn — associating it with the poverty and squalor of the Irish — during the early nineteenth century, even they were forced to consider the potato as an alternative to grains. When for several consecutive years the wheat crop failed, the government attempted to change people's attitude towards the potato. The aristocracy remained unaffected, but the poor had to learn to accept it. At first it was consumed mainly in the form of potato flour, but gradually by the middle of the century the potato had become the major source of food for the working class.

In 1664 the Englishman John Foster wrote a work entitled ''England's Happiness Increased, or a Sure and Easy Remedy Against All Succeeding Dear Years by a Plantation of Roots Called Potatoes.'' In spite of its enthusiastic title and moral implications, it probably was not a best-seller. By 1845, the entire population of Ireland and most of the lower classes in England had become dependent on the potato. However, because potatoes were not yet scientifically bred (perhaps because they were the diet of only the poor), the potato was a constant victim of disease and the weather. In Ireland, the potato crop had failed, for one reason or another, over twenty times in the eighteenth and early nineteenth centuries. In the great famine years, 1845-47, when blight hit the potato crops, the results were devastating. Millions were left without food of any kind. The Irish had no food alternatives — a million Irish starved to death, and a million more emigrated to America.

If the Irish adopted the potato of necessity and the English held it in contempt as long as possible, how did it fare in the rest of Europe?

For the most part the potato excited suspicion and animosity. Some fashionable aristocrats valued the plant as an ornament and cultivated the flowers, but they were not keen on putting the tubers into their mouths. In 1619 potatoes were banned in Burgundy for causing leprosy; in Switzerland they were associated with scrofula (a swelling of the glands). Thus vilified, the potato became something of a rarity in most of Europe; but as a result, it acquired another reputation: as an aphrodisiac. Like the rare rhinoceros horn, the potato was supposed to enhance the deed of darkness. It was said, "Eating of these roots doth excite Venus and increaseth lust." No doubt there were secret potato societies, black market potato purveyors, suspicious and exotic characters peddling potato powder or potato ointment. Who knew what secret powers lay behind the inscrutable potato exterior?

However, the potato did have its champions. Frederick the Great of Prussia encouraged its cultivation and persuaded his subjects to accept it as food. He was so successful that the first potato recipes appeared in German in *Ein Neu Kochbuch,* published in 1581. Today the East Germans are the world's champion potato eaters with an annual per capita consumption of more than 370 pounds (168 kg).

In the late eighteenth century Antoine-Auguste Parmentier, a French agriculturalist who took a special interest in potatoes, wrote "Inquiry Into Nourishing Vegetables That in Times of Necessity Could Be Substituted for Ordinary Food." Parmentier wanted to rid the potato of its reputation as at best an ornament and at worst a carrier of disease.

Convincing King Louis XVI of the need to plant a potato patch, Parmentier devised a ruse to whet the curiosity of the locals. He posted soldiers during the day to guard the patch; at night he removed the sentries. People, assuming the soldiers were guarding something of great value, raided the garden at night. One wonders what they thought when they plucked the tubers from the soil. However, Parmentier was successful in generating interest in the plant, and to this day his name is synonymous with potato cookery in France.

Today, more than 5,000 strains of potato exist in research laboratories. There are some 2,000 varieties of the potato family grown around the world, but only a few of the known varieties are grown commercially in each region. Some species of the potato grow in the cold, mountain climate of the Andes. Others have been developed to suit the humid climate of the tropics in places such as the Philippines and Vietnam. In Canada, the town of Cochrane, situated well inside the northern frontier, claims to be the potato capital of the world.

It's not surprising to learn that the Soviet Union produces about a quarter of the world's potatoes. On a recent trip to the Soviet Union we were served potatoes, in one form or another, at every meal. Potatoes are ideal for the Soviet diet: they cultivate well in northern climates, can be stored through the long winters and their adaptable flavour and texture combine well with traditional, local cuisines. In fact, potatoes seem so much a part of the cuisines of Central Europe and the Soviet Union that it's difficult to keep in mind that they are relative newcomers. In just over a century, the potato has gone from being an exotic food to taking a central role in the diets of Europeans and many Asians. Indian cookery, in particular, makes good use of the versatile potato.

This book has been designed to reflect the potato's widespread acceptance, with recipes from many parts of the world, but the dishes are easy to prepare and don't require expensive or inaccessible ingredients. While potatoes are used to make everything from fake snow to alcohol, our intention is not to dazzle you with the many faces of the potato, but rather, to give practical recipes which make the most of its special food qualities. There are traditional and new recipes — from soups and salads, through main courses and side dishes to snacks — that show off the potato's ability to absorb flavours, thicken liquids and add decorative touches. We celebrate the noble spud and reveal it in all its glory as one of the most nutrient-rich, economical and versatile foods we have.

VARIETIES

Although all potatoes have certain important properties in common, different varieties have been specially cultivated to meet the needs of regional growing conditions and cuisines. Each area produces numerous varieties, but the number available in the stores is generally only about four. Each type has its own cooking qualities, and although the specific name may not be quite the same, you will recognize its characteristics.

Four Main Types Available in North America

Russet or Idaho type — long and flat, with round ends

Characteristics:	Brown, rough, dry, relatively thick skin
	Whitish flesh
	Dry, mealy texture
	High starch, low moisture content

Best for:	Baking
	Deep frying
	Mashing
	Barbecues
	Soups
	Scones, cakes, breads

Red Rounds — smallish and round, with deep eyes

Characteristics:	Thin, smooth, red/purple skins
	Creamy white flesh
	Moist, firm, waxy texture
	High moisture, low starch content

Best for:	Boiling
	Steaming
	Salads

Large White Ovals — long and oval, with pointed ends

Characteristics:	Thin, smooth, creamy-beige skin, few eyes
	Waxy, firm texture

Best for:	Boiling
	Pan frying
	Deep frying
	Mashing
	Grating and shredding
	Soups
	Curries
	Stews and casseroles

White Rounds — smallish and round

Characteristics:	Smooth, beige skin
	Creamy flesh
	Moist, waxy, firm texture
	High moisture, low starch content
Best for:	Boiling
	Stewing
	Braising
	Salads

There are several grades available in each of these types. The grade is determined by the quality of the skin, number of eyes and regularity of the shape. Misshapen potatoes are difficult to handle, grade and prepare, and so rarely find their way onto the market.

New Potatoes

These are not a special type of potato, but young tubers gathered before the crop is mature and before the enzymes have converted sugar into starch. They are small with a delicate, almost transparent skin and high moisture content which gives a waxy texture. They don't keep longer than about a week.

New potatoes are seen in our northern markets for only a few weeks each year. Depending on the climate, there are usually three potato crops during the year — early, main crop and late potatoes.

New potatoes are especially good for simple preparations such as boiling and are perfect for potato salads — either hot or cold. New potatoes should be placed directly into boiling water, not cold water. They are the exception to the rule that root vegetables start in cold water and vegetables that grow above ground go into boiling water.

Four Main Types
Available in the United Kingdom

Home Guard — small, oval/round shape

Characteristics:	Firm, creamy-white flesh
	Smooth skin with few eyes
	Available June to August
Best for:	Boiling
	Salads

Red Craig's Royal — medium-sized, oval shape

Characteristics:	Smooth, red skin with few eyes
	Pale creamy flesh
	Waxy texture
	Available from July onwards
Best for:	Boiling
	Pan frying
	Salads

King Edward — large, oval/round shape

Characteristics:	Roughish, light brown skin with some red markings
	Dry, slightly floury texture
	Available September to April
Best for:	Mashing
	Baking
	Roasting

Majestic — medium to large, oval or kidney-shaped

Characteristics:	Creamy-white skin with shallow eyes
	White flesh
	Available September to April
Best for:	All-purpose
	Deep frying
	Pan frying
	Boiling
	Mashing
	Salads

VITAL STATISTICS

The potato, *Solanum tuberosum,* is a perennial of the nightshade family, but there's no need for alarm. Being kin to the deadly nightshade doesn't make the potato tuber harmful, but it does mean that all green parts of the plant are toxic. Other edible members of this family are tomatoes and eggplants. Potatoes which turn green through exposure to light should not be eaten since the greenness indicates the presence of certain toxic substances under the skin. Eating green potatoes can cause nausea, headaches and stomach cramps.

The potato is not related to the sweet potato or yam, which belongs to a different botanical family. The roots we call sweet potatoes belong to the morning glory family. The major difference is that the sweet potato is a swollen root, whereas the potato is a rhyzome, a tuberous swelling at the tip of a root.

It's interesting that potatoes don't grow from seeds but from sprouting tubers known as seed potatoes. Research is under way to develop potatoes which will grow from seeds since seeds are less perishable and much easier to handle than seed potatoes.

Agricultural research has also led to the wider acceptance of potatoes as a staple around the world. On the basis of yield per unit of land and food value per pound (or kilo) researchers have found that the potato could challenge wheat — the so-called ''staff of life'' — in its importance in the human diet.

NUTRITION

A complex carbohydrate, the potato is now recognized as an important food. Unlike animal protein, fats and concentrated sugars that have wreaked havoc, producing clogged arteries, high blood pressure and digestive problems, complex carbohydrates are regarded as an essential part of a well-balanced diet. A potato contains far greater food value than an equal quantity of steak, but it has three times *fewer* calories. Yet, when we diet, it's common practice to cut out potatoes in favour of the steak. What we overlook is the fat that comes along with the meat — I don't mean the large pieces of fat which might be cut away and discarded, but the fat that is incorporated in the tissues of the meat, giving the meat its flavour. Potatoes contain none of these hidden liabilities.

A nutritionally important food gives a good return on its calories; that is, there are many nutrients per calorie. On this score, there can be no question that a potato gives you your money's worth of nutrients. The accompanying table shows what food value there is in an average potato. For a dieter it's not the potato but the accompanying sour cream, butter or oil that does the damage. In fact, a potato-a-day could supplant the apple-a-day as an ideal source of nutrients. In addition, potatoes are cheaper per pound than any other fruit or vegetable, and because of their adaptable nature, there are hundreds of ways to cook them.

Along with these important nutrients, potatoes give us fibre, often called roughage. Although we don't digest fibre, it's important for maintaining a healthy digestive system.

Major Nutrients in a Medium Potato Baked in its Skin

Weight	100 g	Weight	100 g
Moisture	75%	Sodium	4 mg
Calories	91	Potassium	503 mg
Protein	3 g	Vitamin A	trace
Carbohydrate	21 g	Thiamin	.10 mg
Fat	trace	Riboflavin	.04 mg
Cholesterol	0 mg	Niacin	1.7 NE
Calcium	9 mg	Folate	14 mcg
Iron	0.7 mg	Vitamin C	20 mg

Source: Department of Health and Welfare Canada

STORAGE

Potatoes keep well in a cool, dark, slightly humid place with good ventilation. They will begin to sprout and shrivel if the temperature is over 50°F (10°C), and a refrigerator is too cold and moist for them.

Ideal storage temperatures are between 45°F (8°C) and 50°F (10°C). You may be able to keep home-grown potatoes for months but, since the age of potatoes bought in a store is unknown, don't plan on keeping them for more than a few weeks, no matter how well they're stored. New potatoes keep about one week.

When potatoes are exposed to light, they gradually become green; this is caused by a toxic substance under the skin. All green parts should be completely cut away, and if the whole potato becomes green it should be thrown out.

Once bought, potatoes should be removed from any plastic bags and stored loosely in a vegetable bin, sack or brown paper bag.

Potatoes and onions should not be stored together because the natural gases given off by each of these vegetables will affect their keeping abilities.

METHODS OF COOKING

Boiling
Mature potatoes should be cleaned by brushing with a firm brush under running water. It's best to boil them unpeeled to retain the many nutrients stored just under the skin. Potatoes can lose about one-third of their food value if they are peeled before they are cooked. You'll find that the skins come off easily after they have been boiled, and a great deal more of the potato's flesh can be retained as well.

Potatoes should be just covered with cold, lightly salted water and brought to the boil. Continue to boil, uncovered, until the potatoes are tender when pierced with a fork. Cooking time depends on the size of the potato, but the average potato cooks in about 20 minutes. All potatoes cooked together should be roughly the same size so that they will cook in the same time. Cut any large potatoes into chunks to even out the sizes. A few sprigs of fresh mint in the water adds to the flavour.

Once potatoes have boiled, drain them immediately and return them to the pot. Toss them gently over moderate heat to remove excess moisture. Butter and extra salt may be added at this stage. If you notice any dark spots on the stem end of a boiled potato, it indicates a concentration of iron. An addition of a little lemon juice to the cooking water will prevent the oxidization that causes the darkening.

Parboiling
This involves boiling the potatoes for about 10 minutes to speed their cooking if you plan to roast, pan fry or deep fry them afterwards.

Steaming
Potatoes take considerably longer to cook when they are steamed, but they retain more of their food value and stay firmer. Place the potatoes on a wire rack or colander inside a large saucepan and add only enough boiling water to come up to the level of the rack. Cover with a tight-fitting lid to keep in the steam. You may need to add a little more water from time to time.

Braising
Potatoes may be braised in a covered pan on top of the stove or in the oven. Braising is a combination of boiling and frying or roasting

and gives an excellent flavour, particularly if you use a little stock instead of water.

To braise, cut potatoes into even-sized pieces and fry briefly over moderate heat in a little butter or oil. Add a cup (250 mL) of water or stock, a teaspoon (5 mL) of salt and seasonings such as minced garlic, grated onion or fresh herbs. Cover tightly and cook over moderate heat for 35–40 minutes or until tender. If you braise in the oven, use an oven-proof dish with a tight-fitting lid and add at least 15 minutes to the cooking time. You may need to add more liquid as the potatoes cook, depending on how tightly the lid fits.

Baking

Details for baking are given in the recipe section for baked potatoes, but here are a few important rules to follow. Choose mealy textured baking potatoes — Russet, Netted Gems or Idaho potatoes are common baking varieties. Clean the potatoes and dry them thoroughly. Prick the skins with a fork but do not wrap them in foil; potatoes wrapped in foil will steam as the potato's own moisture builds up under the foil. Compare a potato baked in foil with one baked without foil and you will notice a difference in texture and flavour. A baked potato should have a fluffy texture rather than the moist, firm texture produced by wrapping. Rub the skins with a little butter or oil, but if you want a crisp skin, the butter or oil isn't necessary.

Bake in the oven at 400°F (200°C) for about one hour or until the potatoes are soft when pressed with the fingers. Once the potatoes have cooked, remove from the oven and cut a deep X along the top of each potato. Press in the sides to loosen the pulp and open the cut in the top. You may want to insert butter, sour cream or seasonings into the opening.

Potatoes can be baked on the barbecue either whole or in wedges. Prepare the wedges by parboiling them for about 10 minutes. Drain them and toss them in seasoned oil, then place them on the barbecue along with the steaks or hamburgers. Whole potatoes can be prepared and cooked in the same way, but they will take longer to cook and the skin will be charred. If you prefer uncharred skin, wrap the potatoes in foil and place them directly in the coals.

Oven Roasting

Oven-roasted potatoes take about an hour to cook, but you can reduce the time in the oven by first parboiling them for about 10 minutes.

Oven-roasted potatoes are usually peeled, although this is more a custom than a necessity. Cut potatoes in halves or even thirds if they are large. Arrange them in a shallow baking pan and coat them with a little oil. My mother uses a well-flavoured dripping instead of oil, and her roast potatoes are undoubtedly the best in the world.

Usually the potatoes are cooked along with a roast of meat which adds the flavour of its pan juices. Potatoes should be added to the meat during the last hour and a half of cooking. (They cook a little faster if they are on their own.) Whether cooked with meat or on their own, the potatoes should be turned occasionally to brown on all sides.

FREEZING

While frozen French fries occupy a prime position in the freezer section of your local supermarket, potatoes prepared in other ways generally don't freeze well.

If you freeze home-made French fries or chips, deep fry them in clean oil until they have turned a light golden colour. They should be drained, cooled and spread on a baking sheet with a little air space left around each fry.

Freeze the fries on the open tray until they are hard, then transfer them to a plastic bag for long-term freezing. Fries frozen this way should keep up to 6 months.

When it's time to serve them, it's better to re-fry them while still frozen, rather than allowing them to thaw. Although the hot oil will spit when you immerse the frozen fries, thawing causes sogginess. Be *very* careful when you fry them.

Croquettes, dumplings, fritters and pancakes may be frozen for up to 3 months. Use the method recommended for French fries, freezing the items singly before you package them for long-term freezing. These items should also be reheated without first thawing.

Dishes with mashed-potato toppings, such as Shepherd's Pie, can be prepared as usual, then transferred to a foil or freezer container, cooled, wrapped firmly and frozen. If the dishes include bacon, sausages, ham or pork, they should keep for about 6 weeks; otherwise they'll keep for about 3 months. Casseroles such as these should be reheated slowly from the frozen state.

SOUPS AND SALADS

Hot and Cold Delight of Potatoes

The versatile potato is an ideal addition to any soup. Cut into chunks or diced, potatoes add substance to hearty soups and act as the perfect carrier of flavours. Mashed potatoes make an easy and tasty thickener for soups. An even better way is to cook the potatoes along with other vegetables — carrots, zucchini or cauliflower — and purée them to make a thick, rich, satisfying soup.

When you make potato salads, use potatoes that are freshly cooked and still warm. Warm potatoes absorb more flavour from the other ingredients than cold potatoes.

Mayonnaise blends beautifully with potatoes and lays the foundation of a traditional potato salad. But a blend of sour cream, vinegar and a little sugar makes a fine alternative to mayonnaise, and yoghurt mixed with herbs, sunflower seeds or chopped nuts is a nutritious substitute. Hot potato salads are popular in central and northern Europe and are usually served along with the main course.

Soups

Red Potato Soup, 23
Scots Potato Soup, 24
Potato-Asparagus Soup, 25
Creamy Potato Soup, 26
Cressonnière, 27
Curried Potato Soup, 28
Clam Chowder, 29
New York Chowder, 30
Aussie Chowder, 31
Low-cal Potato Soup, 32
Lithuanian Potato Soup, 33
Kalamojakka — Fish and Potato Soup, 34
Garlic and Potato Soup, 35
Vichyssoise, 36
Potage Parmentier, 36
Potato-Cheddar Soup, 37
Potato-Sunroot Soup, 38
Rosy Potato Soup, 40
Zucchini-Potato Soup, 41

Salads

Crunchy Curried Potato Salad, 42
Hot Shrimp and Potato Salad, 43
New World Potato Salad, 44
Hot or Cold Potato Salad, 45
Mediterranean Salad, 46
Anchovy-Potato Salad, 47
Potato and Herring Salad, 48
Ham and Potato Salad, 49
Mexican Bean and Potato Salad, 50
Sillisalatti, 51
Aloo Raita, 52
Shaker Salad, 53
Clare's Salad, 54

RED POTATO SOUP

This substantial soup is rich, red and piquant. You can use a vegetable stock if you prefer, but this Hungarian-style soup tastes best made with either beef or chicken stock.

Leeks	3
Butter	3 Tbsp (50 mL)
Flour	3 Tbsp (50 mL)
Stock	6 cups (1.5 L)
Potatoes	4 medium, peeled and coarsely chopped
Tomatoes	4 medium, peeled and seeded
Tomato paste	2 Tbsp (25 mL)
Salt	1/2 tsp (2 mL)
Pepper	1/4 tsp (1 mL)
Hungarian paprika	1 tsp (5 mL)
Sour cream	1/2 cup (125 mL)
Green onions	4, trimmed and chopped

1 Trim off the rough green sections of the leeks, retaining only the white interior leaves and the tenderest green parts. Cut off the root. With a sharp knife, slice the leeks in half lengthwise to expose the inner leaves. Hold under running water and separate the leaves to wash out all the grit that clings to them. Chop the leeks coarsely.

2 Melt the butter in a large pot. Add the chopped leeks and coat well with butter. Cover the pot and sweat the leeks for about 15 minutes. Remove the pot from the heat.

3 Add the flour to the leeks and blend well with a wooden spoon. Return to the heat and cook briefly until the flour begins to turn golden. Add the stock, a little at a time, and continue to stir, making sure the liquid blends in well.

4 Add the potatoes, tomatoes, tomato paste, salt, pepper and paprika. Bring to a boil and continue to cook over moderate heat for 1/2 an hour. Set aside and allow to cool a little.

5 Purée the soup, a small batch at a time, in a food mill or food processor.

6 Reheat and serve topped with sour cream and chopped green onions.

Serves 6

SCOTS POTATO SOUP

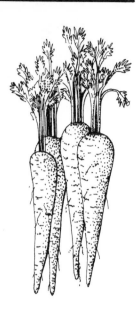

This recipe is traditionally made with mutton, but I've suggested chicken here since mutton can be difficult to find. If you use mutton, the taste will be quite different. Place the mutton in a shallow pan with about 2 cups (500 mL) of water and a couple of small onions and cook in a moderate oven for about 1 1/2 hours. Then remove the pan from the oven, skim off the fat, add the vegetables and return the pan to the oven for further cooking. Then follow the instructions below, starting at step two.

Potatoes	3 large
Onions	2 medium
Carrots	2 medium, cleaned
Whole chicken	1 medium
Water or stock	6 cups (1.5 L)
Dried sage	1/2 tsp (2 mL)
Salt	1/2 tsp (2 mL)
Pepper	a pinch
Fresh parsley	3 Tbsp (50 mL) finely chopped

Preheat oven to 350°F (180°C).

1 Peel the potatoes and onions and chop coarsely. Slice the carrots into even-sized slices. Rinse the chicken and remove the giblets from the cavity.

2 Combine all the ingredients (except one half of the parsley for garnish) in a large, heavy, oven-proof pot. Cover and cook in a moderate oven (350°F, 180°C) for about 1 1/4 hours.

3 When the chicken is cooked, lift it onto a platter. Strain the liquid from the pot and reserve it. Set aside the strained vegetables with the chicken.

4 Allow the liquid from the pot to cool and skim off the fat.

5 Purée the vegetables in a food mill or food processor and return them to the pot.

6 Skin and bone the chicken and cut the flesh into bite-sized pieces. Combine the chicken pieces with the vegetables in the pot.

7 Add the reserved liquid to the pot. Reheat on top of the stove and adjust the seasoning. Serve with a garnish of chopped parsley.

Serves 6

POTATO-ASPARAGUS SOUP

This soup may be served cold or hot. Once the asparagus has been added, don't let it cook too long or it will lose its fresh, green colour.

Potatoes	6 medium, peeled and diced
Onion	1 medium, peeled and finely chopped
Chicken stock	8 cups (2 L)
Salt	1/2 tsp (2 mL)
Pepper	1/4 tsp (1 mL)
Cayenne	a pinch
Fresh asparagus	2 cups (500 mL) chopped
Butter	1 Tbsp (15 mL)
Fresh dill	1 Tbsp (15 mL) finely chopped
Shallots	1/4 cup (50 mL) chopped
Fresh parsley	1 Tbsp (15 mL) finely chopped
Lemon juice	1 Tbsp (15 mL)
Sour cream	1 cup (250 mL)

1 Place the potatoes and onion in a large pot and cover with the chicken stock. Bring the liquid to a boil and allow to simmer for about 20 minutes.

2 Strain the vegetables, reserving the stock. Purée the vegetables in a food processor or food mill. Recombine and add the salt, pepper and cayenne.

3 Add the asparagus pieces, butter, and about half the chopped dill, shallots and parsley. Reheat and cook gently for 15 minutes.

4 Add the lemon juice and remaining chopped herbs. Stir well.

5 Top each serving with a dollop of sour cream.

Serves 6

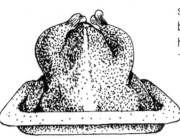

CREAMY POTATO SOUP

The need for a soothing bowl of chicken soup strikes everyone sooner or later. This creamy potato version of chicken soup might be even better than the one mother used to make. If it is, don't tell her about it!

Butter	2 Tbsp (25 mL)
Onion	1 medium, peeled and finely chopped
Chicken stock	3 cups (750 mL)
Potatoes	3 medium, peeled and diced
Milk	2 cups (500 mL)
Flour	1 Tbsp (15 mL)
Salt	1/2 tsp (2 mL)
Pepper	to taste
Cooked chicken	1 1/2 cups (375 mL) diced
Fresh parsley and chives	1 Tbsp (15 mL) finely chopped

1 Melt the butter in a large pot. Add the chopped onions and sweat them gently for about 7 minutes or until they become transparent.

2 Add the chicken stock and diced potatoes. Cover and cook over moderate heat for about 20 minutes. Remove the pot from the heat.

3 Mix a little milk with the flour to make a smooth paste and press out any lumps of flour. Combine the floury paste with the rest of the milk, then add the mixture to the pot. Stir well and add the salt and pepper to taste.

4 Reheat the soup to boiling and stir well as it thickens. When the soup comes to a boil, add the diced chicken and cook for another five minutes over moderate heat, stirring occasionally.

5 Mix in the fresh chopped herbs just before serving.

Serves 4

CRESSONNIÈRE

Cressonnière is delightfully fresh served cold in the summer, topped with chopped chives. In the winter, served hot with croutons, it makes a hearty fireside meal.

Leeks	2
Butter	1 Tbsp (15 mL)
Chicken stock	4 cups (1 L)
Potatoes	4 large, peeled and diced
Bouquet garni	1 sachet (approximately 1 tsp or 5 mL)
Salt	1/2 tsp (2 mL)
Watercress	1/2 cup (125 mL) finely chopped
Fresh parsley	1 Tbsp (15 mL) finely chopped

Croutons

Stale bread	3 slices, trimmed and diced
Butter	2 Tbsp (25 mL)

1 Trim off the rough, green sections of the leeks, retaining only the white interior leaves and the tenderest green parts. Cut off the root. With a sharp knife, slice the leeks in half lengthwise to expose the inner leaves. Hold under running water and separate the leaves to wash out all the grit that clings to them. Chop the leeks coarsely.

2 In a large, heavy saucepan melt the butter and add the chopped leeks. Cover and cook gently for 10 minutes.

3 Add the stock and diced potatoes along with the bouquet garni. Bring to a boil. Skim off any froth on the surface. Simmer for 20 minutes, then add the salt and chopped watercress. Simmer for another 15 minutes. Remove from the heat.

4 Remove the bouquet garni. Add the parsley and purée the soup in a food mill or food processor.

5 Return the soup to the saucepan and reheat. Serve topped with croutons.

6 To make croutons, melt the butter in a large frying pan. When the foam subsides, add the diced bread and fry until crisp. Drain well on paper towels.

Serves 6

CURRIED POTATO SOUP

Mashed potatoes work well as a thickening agent for many soups and stews. In this soup, the potato also carries the flavour of the curry.

Butter	1 Tbsp (15 mL)
Onion	1 medium, finely chopped
Mild curry powder	2 tsp (10 mL)
Apple	1 large, peeled and grated
Chutney, optional	1 Tbsp (15 mL)
Chicken stock	3 cups (750 mL)
Mashed potatoes	2 cups (500 mL)
Cooked chicken	1 cup (250 mL) diced
Salt	1 tsp (5 mL)
Pepper	1/2 tsp (2 mL)
Milk	1 cup (250 mL)

1 In a large saucepan melt the butter and fry the chopped onions, curry powder and apple for about 3 minutes.

2 Add the chutney and mix through. Add the chicken stock and bring the soup to a boil.

3 Add the mashed potatoes, diced chicken, and salt and pepper. Stir through. Add the milk and simmer gently for 10 minutes.

Serves 4

CLAM CHOWDER

Unlike some vegetable and meat soups, clam and other seafood soups don't improve with keeping. They should be served as soon as they are made.

Butter	1 Tbsp (15 mL)
Onions	2, peeled and finely chopped
Clams	2 cans, 5-oz (142-g)
Potatoes	4 large, peeled and diced small
Evaporated milk	1 can, 14-oz (390-mL)
Salt	1 tsp (5 mL)
White pepper	1/4 tsp (1 mL)
Cayenne	1/4 tsp (1 mL)
Fresh parsley	1 Tbsp (15 mL) finely chopped

1 Melt the butter in a large pot. Add the onions and fry over moderate heat until transparent but not brown.

2 Drain the juice from both cans of clams into the pot and set aside the clams. Add the diced potatoes, then cover and cook for 15 minutes. (Add a little water if there is not enough clam juice to cover the potatoes.)

3 Add the evaporated milk, salt, pepper and cayenne and simmer for another 15 minutes.

4 Add the clams and cook gently for about 3 minutes. Top with chopped parsley and serve immediately.

Serves 4

NEW YORK CHOWDER

The chowders called "Manhattan" or "New York" are distinguished by the addition of tomato in one form or another. Of course, if you can get fresh clams, use them instead of the canned. Clean and steam them and remove the shells. Add them to the soup during the last few minutes of cooking.

Leeks	2
Butter	2 Tbsp (25 mL)
Onions	3 medium, peeled and finely chopped
Celery	2 stalks including leaves, finely chopped
Clams	2 cans, 5-oz (142-g)
Chicken stock	4 cups (1 L)
Potatoes	3 large, peeled and diced
Bouquet garni	1 sachet
Bay leaf	1
Salt	1/2 tsp (2 mL)
Pepper	1/2 tsp (2 mL)
Whole tomatoes	1 can, 28-oz (796-mL)
Sherry	1 Tbsp (15 mL)
Fresh Italian parsley	1/2 cup (125 mL) finely chopped

1 Trim off the rough, green sections of the leeks, retaining only the white interior leaves and the tenderest green parts. Cut off the root. With a sharp knife, slice the leeks in half lengthwise to expose the inner leaves. Hold under running water and separate the leaves to wash out all the grit that clings to them. Chop the leeks coarsely.

2 Melt the butter in a large saucepan. Add the onions, leeks and celery. Cover and sweat them gently for about 20 minutes.

3 Strain the juice from the clams and add it to the saucepan, along with the stock, diced potatoes, bouquet garni, bay leaf, salt and pepper. Cover and bring to a boil, then simmer for 30 minutes.

4 Drain the tomatoes and chop finely. Add the tomatoes, sherry and clams to the soup and bring it back to a boil. Add the parsley and stir it through. Serve immediately.

Serves 4-6

AUSSIE CHOWDER

I grew up by the sea, and my father's hobby was fishing — in the open sea, in salt water lakes and in the tidal river close to our house — so I came by my love of seafood honestly. We caught prawns (shrimp) and collected oysters and even abalone, as well as fish. And from time to time these seafoods all came together in this Aussie chowder.

Butter	1 Tbsp (15mL)
Onions	2, peeled and finely chopped
Potatoes	4 large, peeled and diced
Salt	1 tsp (5 mL)
Garlic	1 clove, minced
Fish stock	5 cups (1.25 L)
Firm-fleshed fish	1 lb (450 g), trimmed and scaled
Raw shrimp	1 dozen, peeled
Scallops	6, shelled and bearded
Oysters	1 dozen, shelled
Cream	1 cup (250 mL)
Fresh parsley	2 Tbsp (25 mL) finely chopped

1 In a large pot melt the butter and add the chopped onions. Fry over medium heat for 5 minutes or until the onions become transparent.

2 Add the potatoes, salt, minced garlic and fish stock. Bring to a boil, then reduce the heat and cook gently for 10 minutes.

3 Cut the fish into chunks but do not de-bone. Add the fish to the stock and cook gently for 10 minutes longer. Skim off any foam on the surface.

4 Add the shrimp and scallops and cook gently just until the shrimp turn pink.

5 Add the oysters and cook one minute longer. Stir in the cream and parsley. Heat through but do not boil. Serve at once.

Serves 4

LOW-CAL POTATO SOUP

Traditionally potato soups are creamy and, consequently, not diet fare. But this vegetable soup has a clear broth base, making it low in calories and nutritious as well. If you prefer, chicken stock may be substituted for the beef stock suggested here.

Leeks	2
Margarine	1 Tbsp (15 mL)
Onions	2 medium, finely chopped
Potatoes	4 medium
Carrots	2 medium, trimmed and cleaned
Celery	2 stalks
Beef stock	5 cups (1.25 L)
Salt	1/2 tsp (2 mL)
Pepper	1/4 tsp (1 mL)
Fresh parsley	1 Tbsp (15 mL) finely chopped
Fresh chives	1 Tbsp (15 mL) finely chopped

1 Trim off the rough, green sections of the leeks, retaining only the white interior leaves and the tenderest green parts. Cut off the root. With a sharp knife, slice the leeks in half lengthwise to expose the inner leaves. Hold under running water and separate the leaves to wash out all the grit that clings to them. Chop the leeks coarsely.

2 Melt the margarine in a large soup pot. Add the chopped leeks and onions and sweat gently for 10 minutes.

3 Peel the potatoes and cut into small dice — about 1/2 inch (1.25 cm).

4 Dice the carrots and chop the celery approximately the same size as the potatoes.

5 Add all the vegetables to the pot and pour in the stock. Bring the soup to a boil. Skim off any foam on top of the soup. Reduce the heat, cover and simmer for about 35 minutes. Season with salt and pepper.

6 Serve topped with generous amounts of chopped parsley and chives.

Serves 6

Top: Anchovy Frittata (see page 60)
Bottom: Mediterranean Salad (see page 46)

LITHUANIAN POTATO SOUP

This recipe calls for sorrel, which may be a little difficult to find, but it's worth looking for in specialty stores or farmer's markets. There are no substitutes for the distinctive acid flavour of sorrel. If you cannot get it, you may use watercress or parsley instead, but the flavour will be quite different.

Potatoes	4 medium, boiled and peeled
Garlic	1 clove, minced
Sorrel	1 Tbsp (15 mL) finely chopped
Celery	2 stalks, finely chopped
Salt	1/2 tsp (2 mL)
Pepper	1/4 tsp (1 mL)
Small pork sausages	1 lb (450 g)
Chicken stock	3 cups (750 mL)
Cream	1/2 cup (125 mL)
Eggs	3, hard-boiled
Fresh chives	1 Tbsp (15 mL) finely chopped

1   With an electric beater pureé the potatoes. Add the minced garlic, sorrel, celery, salt and pepper. Transfer to a large soup pot and set aside.

2   In a frying pan fry the sausages for approximately 8 minutes, turning them to brown evenly. Drain off the excess fat. Pat the sausages with paper towels to remove surface grease.

3   Add the chicken stock and sausages to the puréed potato mixture. Stir through. Bring the soup to a boil. Reduce the heat and simmer for 10 minutes. Add the cream and stir through.

4   Peel and finely chop the hard-boiled eggs. Garnish each serving of soup with the chopped eggs and chives.

Serves 4

KALAMOJAKKA – FISH AND POTATO SOUP

This soup is called *kalakeitto* in Finland, but the word used by many North American Finns is *kalamojakka*. It's reminiscent of northern forests and lakes. Rick remembers his grandfather's freshly caught pike or pickerel magically transformed with potatoes, onions, allspice and dill into this succulent soup — a meal in itself. Although you can use any white-fleshed freshwater fish, we recommend some fine salmon. Make a winter afternoon come to life with soup and homemade potato bread.

Salmon	1 1/2 lbs (675–700 g)
Onion	1 large, coarsely chopped
Salt	1 Tbsp (15 mL)
Allspice	6 whole
Water	4 cups (1 L)
Potatoes	6–8 small
Milk	3 cups (750 mL)
Butter	2 Tbsp (25 mL)
Fresh dill	3 Tbsp (50 mL) finely chopped

1 Cut the salmon into chunks and put into a heavy pot with the onion, salt and allspice. Add the water, cover and simmer slowly.

2 Peel and quarter the potatoes and put them into another pot.

3 Just as the simmering fish becomes flaky, drain off the stock into the potato pot. Take care not to let the fish become mushy. Leave the fish in the pot and set it aside.

4 Cook the potatoes until they are soft yet firm, then pour the potatoes and the stock into the pot containing the fish. Add the milk and simmer gently for 15 minutes.

5 Garnish with butter and dill before serving.

Serves 4

GARLIC AND POTATO SOUP

Leeks	2 large
Butter	3 Tbsp (50 mL)
Potatoes	4 large, peeled and cubed
Milk	3 cups (750 mL)
Chicken or vegetable stock	3 cups (750 mL)
Garlic	3 cloves, minced
Salt	1 tsp (5 mL)
Ground nutmeg	1/4 tsp (1 mL)
Croutons	2 cups (500 mL) (see recipe for Cressonnière)

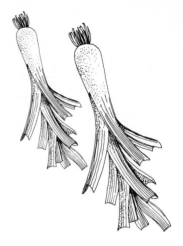

1 Trim off the rough, green sections of the leeks, retaining only the white interior leaves and the tenderest green parts. Cut off the root. With a sharp knife, slice the leeks in half lengthwise to expose the inner leaves. Hold under running water and separate the leaves to wash out all the grit that clings to them. Chop the leeks coarsely.

2 Melt the butter in a large pot and add the leeks. Cover and sweat the leeks over low heat for about 20 minutes.

3 Add the potatoes, milk, stock and minced garlic. Cook gently for about 25 minutes. Add the salt and nutmeg.

4 Transfer to a food mill or a food processor and purée until smooth. Reheat and serve garnished with croutons.

Serves 6

VICHYSSOISE

This famous cold soup is the North American version of Potage Parmentier. It's so easy to make, and the combination of potato and leek is one of the few examples of man improving on nature. This tastes best if made the day before.

Leeks	4
Butter	2 Tbsp (25 mL)
Onion	1, peeled and coarsely chopped
Salt	1 tsp (5 mL)
White pepper	1/2 tsp (2 mL)
Potatoes	4
Chicken stock	5 cups (1.25 L)
Cream	1/2 cup (125 mL)
Fresh chives	2 Tbsp (25 mL) finely chopped

1 Trim off the rough green sections of the leeks, retaining only the white interior leaves and the tenderest green parts. Cut off the root. With a sharp knife, slice the leeks in half lengthwise to expose the inner leaves. Hold under running water and separate the leaves to wash out all the grit that clings to them. Chop the leeks coarsely.

2 Melt the butter in a large saucepan. Add the leeks and chopped onion, cover and sweat them over low heat for about 20 minutes. Add the salt and pepper.

3 Peel the potatoes and cut them into even-sized pieces. Add them to the leeks. Pour in the chicken stock, bring to a boil, then reduce the heat and simmer for about 45 minutes.

4 Purée the mixture in a food mill or processor. Chill in the refrigerator for several hours, overnight if possible.

5 Top each serving with a little cream and chopped chives.

Serves 4

POTAGE PARMENTIER

The French had been making this soup long before American know-how turned it into vichyssoise. Potage Parmentier, named for the French champion of the potato, Antoine-Auguste Parmentier, is the very same recipe as vichyssoise, except that it's served hot.

POTATO-CHEDDAR SOUP

When one of the soup manufacturers first came up with a cheese soup, I remember doing an imitation of someone seized in the grip of hemlock — yech! But later I discovered this recipe for a rich, creamy cheese soup and was instantly won over.

Potatoes	6 large, peeled and diced
Water or stock	6 cups (1.5 L)
Butter	3 Tbsp (50 mL)
Milk	1 cup (250 mL)
Garlic	2 cloves, peeled
Green onions	3, finely chopped
Cayenne	1/4 tsp (1 mL)
Salt	1 tsp (5 mL)
Sharp Cheddar cheese	1 cup (250 mL) grated
Fresh chives	3 Tbsp (50 mL) finely chopped

1 Put the diced potatoes into a large pot and add the water or stock and butter. Cover and bring to a boil and cook over medium heat for about 30 minutes.

2 While the potatoes are cooking, heat the milk in a small saucepan. Add the garlic cloves and simmer in the milk for 20 minutes.

3 Add the milk and garlic, along with the green onions, cayenne and salt to the potatoes in the pot. Cook, uncovered, for 5 minutes over gentle heat. Remove from the heat. Pass through a food mill or a sieve or purée in a food processor, a small batch at a time.

4 Return the soup to the pot. Add the grated cheese and stir through. Reheat until the cheese has melted. Serve with a garnish of chopped chives.

Serves 6-8

POTATO-SUNROOT SOUP

The Jerusalem artichoke, or sunroot, is one of the few truly indigenous Canadian vegetables. Despite its name, it is neither from Jerusalem nor is it an artichoke.

To me, the name "sunroot" seems particularly appropriate because their large yellow flowers bobbed in the sun in our backyard in Australia. Each Sunday, when the vegetable was in season, my mother's dinner included roasted potatoes and sunroot — although we called them artichokes. Even now, its waxy flesh and nutty flavour can transport me across the 12,000 miles and many years to my childhood.

This once-popular vegetable is now generally ignored, but the gnarled tuber resembling ginger root is a tasty vegetable and well worth looking for in farmer's markets or rural vegetable stands. When cooking them, scrub them well but don't attempt to peel their knobbly surface or you'll be at it all day.

Butter	3 Tbsp (50 mL)
Onion	1, peeled and finely chopped
Waxy potatoes	4, scrubbed and diced
Sunroot (Jerusalem artichoke)	4 roots, scrubbed and diced
Flour	1 Tbsp (15 mL)
Milk	2 cups (500 mL)
Chicken stock	4 cups (1 L)
Celery	2 stalks, finely chopped
Salt	1/2 tsp (2 mL)
Pepper	1/4 tsp (1 mL)
Green onions	1/2 cup finely chopped

1 Melt 2 Tbsp (25 mL) of the butter in a large saucepan. When the foam subsides, fry the chopped onions gently for about 5 minutes.

2 Add the diced potatoes and sunroot and toss in the butter for a few minutes. Spoon the vegetables into a dish and set aside.

3 Melt the remaining butter in the saucepan. Add the flour and blend into the butter. Cook gently until the texture and colour resemble sand. Gradually add the milk, beating it into the flour mixture with a large spoon to keep the mixture smooth. Allow the mixture to thicken and add the stock, incorporating it well. Add the diced potatoes and sunroot and the chopped celery. Bring to a boil. Reduce the heat and cook gently for about 25 minutes. Add salt, pepper and the chopped green onions. Cook for another 5 minutes. Serve hot.

Serves 4

ROSY POTATO SOUP

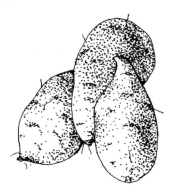

One of the special qualities of the potato is that it will take on the colour and absorb the flavour of anything it's cooked with. Add to that the smooth texture of this noble tuber, and you have a perfect base for soups of all kinds. In this recipe we've combined the potato with a few other root vegetables for a full-bodied soup with the pleasantly sweet flavour that comes naturally to these earthy vegetables.

Butter	2 Tbsp (25 mL)
Onions	2, peeled and finely chopped
Carrots	3, scraped and diced
Potatoes	3 large, peeled and coarsely chopped
Yam or sweet potato	1, peeled and diced
Garlic	1 clove, minced
Cayenne	1/4 tsp (1 mL)
Fresh dill	1 Tbsp (15 mL) finely chopped, plus sprigs for garnish
Nutmeg	1/4 tsp (1 mL) freshly grated
Chicken stock	6 cups (1.5 L)
Salt	1/2 tsp (2 mL)
Sour cream	1/2 cup (125 mL)

1 In a large pot melt the butter and gently sweat the onions and carrots for about 15 minutes.

2 Add the potatoes, yam, garlic, cayenne, dill and nutmeg and sauté in the butter for about 3 minutes.

3 Add the stock and salt and bring the soup to a boil. Reduce the heat, cover and simmer for 30 minutes.

4 Remove from the heat and pour the soup through a sieve. Return the stock to the pot.

5 Purée the vegetables in a food processor or food mill. Add the puréed vegetables to the pot and bring the soup back to a boil. Serve topped with sour cream and sprigs of dill for garnish.

Serves 6

ZUCCHINI-POTATO SOUP

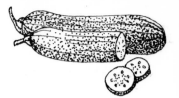

This is a standby in our family because it's hearty, cheap and easy to make. It contains zucchini, but it's really the potato that holds it together.

Potatoes	3 large
Zucchini (courgettes)	4 large
Onions	2 medium
Butter	1 Tbsp (15 mL)
Garlic	1 clove, minced
Chicken stock	6 cups (1.5 L)
Cayenne	1/4 tsp (1 mL)
Salt	1 tsp (5 mL)
Sour cream	1 cup (250 mL)
Fresh chives or parsley	1 Tbsp (15 mL) finely chopped

1 Peel the potatoes and cut them into approximately even-sized pieces.

2 Trim but do not peel the zucchini. Slice them into large, approximately even-sized pieces.

3 Peel the onions and chop them finely.

4 In a large saucepan melt the butter and fry the onions for about 5 minutes. Add the minced garlic, chopped potatoes and zucchini and sauté them in the butter for a few minutes.

5 Add the stock and cayenne and bring to a boil. Reduce the heat, cover and cook gently for about 30 minutes.

6 Add the salt and sour cream and purée in a food processor or food mill.

7 Reheat but do not boil. Serve sprinkled with chopped chives or parsley or a combination of both.

Serves 6

CRUNCHY CURRIED POTATO SALAD

Curry blends beautifully with the creamy texture and flavour of mayonnaise. Add a little leftover diced chicken to this combination to make the classic dish known as Chicken Elizabeth.

Potatoes	5 medium, scrubbed
Butter	1 Tbsp (15 mL)
Onion	1 small, peeled and finely chopped
Mild curry powder	1 1/2 tsp (7 mL)
Apple	1 small
Celery	2 inside stalks
Mayonnaise	1 cup (250 mL)
Raisins	2 Tbsp (25 mL)
Lemon juice	1 Tbsp (15 mL)
Salt	1 tsp (5 mL)
Pepper	1/2 tsp (2 mL)

1 Boil the potatoes in their skins for 20 minutes or until cooked but still firm. Drain and run them under cold water to prevent further cooking.

2 While the potatoes are cooking, melt the butter in a small pan. Add the chopped onions and fry gently until the onions are transparent.

3 Add the curry powder to the onions and blend well into the butter. Cook gently for about 2 minutes to release the curry flavour.

4 Peel and core the apple and if necessary remove the strings from the celery. Dice both coarsely.

5 Coarsely chop the potatoes and put into a large mixing bowl along with the apple and celery, curry mixture and all the remaining ingredients. Mix well but not too vigorously or you will mash the potatoes. Set aside for at least an hour before serving to let the flavours blend.

6 Transfer the salad to a serving dish.

Serves 6

HOT SHRIMP AND POTATO SALAD

I'm always looking for an opportunity to have shrimp, scallops or shell fish of any kind. This salad would be just as good with scallops or a mixture of seafoods.

New potatoes	2 lbs (900 g), uniform sizes
Butter	1 Tbsp (15 mL)
Garlic	1 clove, minced
Raw shrimp	1 lb (450 g), peeled
Water chestnuts	1 can, 10-oz (284-g)
Sour cream	1/2 cup (125 mL)
Oil	1 Tbsp (15 mL)
Cider vinegar	3 Tbsp (50 mL)
Dry mustard	1 tsp (5 mL)
Salt	1/2 tsp (2 mL)
Pepper	1/4 tsp (1 mL)
Fresh dill	1 Tbsp (15 mL) finely chopped
Watercress or fresh dill	for garnish

1 Scrub the potatoes and drop them into boiling water. Cook, uncovered, for about 15–20 minutes, depending on the size. Test with a fork. Drain and run under cold water to prevent further cooking.

2 While the potatoes are cooking, melt the butter in a small frying pan. When the foam subsides, add the minced garlic and peeled shrimp. Cook over moderate heat for approximately 5 minutes or until the shrimp are pink and fairly firm.

3 While the potatoes are still warm, slice them into a large bowl. Pour in the shrimp and pan drippings. Drain and slice the water chestnuts and add to the potatoes.

4 Into the pan used to cook the shrimp pour the sour cream, oil and vinegar. Add the mustard and heat through but do not boil. Pour the mixture over the potatoes and add the salt and pepper. Stir in the chopped dill and garnish with a little watercress or extra dill.

Serves 4

NEW WORLD POTATO SALAD

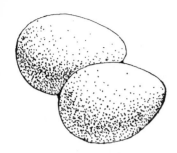

If new potatoes are not available, use any waxy potato. This recipe is shamelessly rich but worth every calorie.

New potatoes	2 lbs (900 g)
Eggs	2, hard-boiled
Red onion	1 large
Sour cream	1 cup (250 mL)
Vinegar	1 Tbsp (15 mL)
Sugar	2 tsp (10 mL)
Salt	1 tsp (5 mL)
Pepper	1/2 tsp (2 mL)
Butter	2 Tbsp (25 mL) melted
Egg yolks	2, well-beaten

1 Wash and boil the potatoes in their skins until just tender. Drain and cut into halves.

2 Peel the hard-boiled eggs and chop into quarters. Peel the onion and chop finely.

3 Mix the potatoes, chopped eggs and onions together in a serving bowl. Keep warm.

4 In a saucepan combine the sour cream, vinegar, sugar, salt, pepper and butter. Heat but do not boil. Remove from the heat and mix in the beaten egg yolks. Heat over a double boiler or a pan of water. Stir the mixture constantly, allowing it to thicken but not to boil. Pour the sauce over the potatoes and serve hot.

Serves 4

HOT OR COLD POTATO SALAD

You can serve this combination of vegetables either hot or cold. I like it hot, served with baked ham.

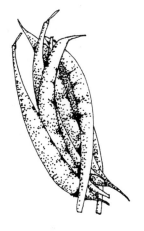

Garlic	1 clove, crushed
Oil	1/4 cup (50 mL)
New potatoes	1 lb (450 g)
Green beans	1/2 lb (225 g)
Water chestnuts	1 can, 10-oz (284-g), drained
Green onions	2, finely chopped
Vinegar	1 Tbsp (15 mL)
Salt	1/2 tsp (2 mL)
Cayenne	1/4 tsp (1 mL)

1 Let the crushed clove of garlic stand in the oil while you prepare the other ingredients.

2 Boil the potatoes in their skins for about 15–20 minutes, until they are cooked but still quite firm. Drain and put them into a large serving bowl. Use an oven-proof bowl if you plan to serve this dish hot.

3 Wash and trim the green beans and steam them for about 5 minutes. Run them under cold water to prevent further cooking.

4 While the beans are cooking, pour the oil and garlic over the potatoes and gently coat the potatoes. Add the cooked beans.

5 Slice the water chestnuts into thin rounds and add them, along with the chopped green onions, to the potatoes. Stir in the vinegar, salt and cayenne.

6 If you are serving this dish hot, cover with foil and warm through in a pre-heated, moderate oven (350°F or 180°C) for 5 minutes.

Serves 4

MEDITERRANEAN SALAD

It's as good as a "beaker full of the warm south," and there's an elegance to this salad with its stylish colours of red, green and white, topped off with glistening black.

New potatoes	2 lbs (900 g), uniform sizes
Tuna	1 can, 6.5-oz (184-g)
Anchovy fillets	1 can, 2-oz (57-g)
Mayonnaise	1/2 cup (125 mL)
Lemon juice	1/3 cup (75 mL)
Pepper	1/2 tsp (2 mL)
Fresh Italian parsley	1/3 cup (75 mL) finely chopped
Red onion	1, thinly sliced
Black olives	10

1 Scrub the potatoes and drop them into boiling water. Cook, uncovered, for approximately 15–20 minutes, depending on the size. Test with a fork and when tender, drain and run them under cold water to prevent further cooking.

2 Into a large bowl drain the liquids from the cans of tuna and anchovy. Set aside the tuna and chop the anchovy fillets, reserving a few whole fillets for garnish. Mix the mayonnaise, lemon juice, pepper, chopped parsley and chopped anchovy into the liquid.

3 Slice the potatoes and place a layer, with slices overlapping, in a large bowl (glass, if you have one). Cover this with a layer of tuna, then a layer of the mayonnaise mixture and a layer of red onion slices.

4 Repeat the layers. Garnish with black olives and anchovy fillets.

Serves 4

ANCHOVY-POTATO SALAD

It's best to make this — or any other potato salad — while the potatoes are still hot or at least warm. Warm potatoes absorb more flavour from the tangy ingredients in this creamy salad.

Potatoes	6 medium
Eggs	4, hard-boiled
Red onion	1 medium, peeled and finely chopped
Fresh parsley	1 Tbsp (15 mL) finely chopped
Fresh chives	1 Tbsp (15 mL) chopped
Salt	1 tsp (5 mL)
Pepper	1/2 tsp (2 mL)
Lemon juice	1 Tbsp (15 mL)
Mayonnaise	1 cup (250 mL)
Anchovy fillets	2 cans, 2-oz (57-g), drained
Capers	12

1 Scrub the potatoes and boil them in their skins for 20 minutes or until cooked but still firm. Drain the potatoes and run them under cold water to prevent further cooking.

2 Peel the eggs and chop them coarsely into a large mixing bowl. Add the chopped onions, parsley, chives, salt and pepper, lemon juice and mayonnaise.

3 Chop the potatoes coarsely into cubes, leaving on the skins. Add to the other ingredients in the bowl and mix thoroughly.

4 Transfer the salad to a large serving bowl. Garnish with anchovy fillets and capers.

Serves 6

POTATO AND HERRING SALAD

When you see dill, herring and sour cream in a recipe, you know it originated somewhere in Scandinavia. Of course, there are regional variations, but this is a traditional Scandinavian potato salad.

Potatoes	6 medium, boiled and diced
Sour cream	4 Tbsp (60 mL)
Fresh dill	1 Tbsp (15 mL) finely chopped
Fresh chives	1 Tbsp (15 mL) finely chopped
Salt	1/2 tsp (2 mL)
Pepper	1/2 tsp (2 mL)
Eggs	3, hard-boiled
Pickled herring	4, cut in strips

1 In a large mixing bowl combine the diced potatoes, sour cream, dill, chives, salt and pepper.

2 Peel the hard-boiled eggs and chop finely.

3 Add the strips of herring and half of the chopped eggs to the potatoes and stir through.

4 Transfer the mixture to a serving dish. Garnish with the remaining chopped eggs.

Serves 6

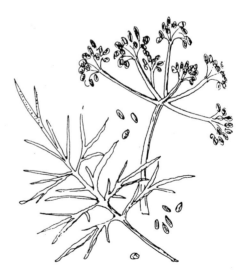

HAM AND POTATO SALAD

Whenever you have leftover ham or turkey, make this hearty potato salad for lunch or supper.

Potatoes	4 medium
Green onion	1 large
Cooked ham	1 cup (250 mL) cubed
Eggs	2, hard-boiled and finely chopped
Mayonnaise	4 Tbsp (60 mL)
Dijon mustard	1 1/2 tsp (7 mL)
Salt	1/2 tsp (2 mL)
Cayenne	1/4 tsp (1 mL)

1 Boil the potatoes in their skins for 20 minutes or until cooked but still firm. Drain and run under cold water to prevent further cooking.

2 Coarsely chop the potatoes into a large bowl. Finely chop the green onion and reserve the green part for garnish.

3 Add the white part of the green onion and the rest of the ingredients to the potatoes. Toss thoroughly and garnish with the remaining green onion.

Serves 4

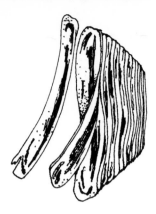

MEXICAN BEAN AND POTATO SALAD

This is one of those salads that can be served either hot or cold. It's especially good with stuffed green peppers or enchiladas.

Potatoes	5 large
Bacon	2 strips, chopped
Onion	1, peeled and chopped
Dried chili pepper	1 tsp (5 mL)
Tabasco sauce	2 drops
Red kidney beans	1 can, 10-oz (250-g)
Lemon juice	1 Tbsp (15 mL)
Salt	1/2 tsp (2 mL)
Pepper	1/4 tsp (1 mL)
Fresh mixed herbs (e.g. chives, basil, parsley, green onions)	2 Tbsp (30 mL) finely chopped

1 Boil the potatoes in their skins and peel them while they are still warm. Cut into thick slices.

2 In a large frying pan cook the bacon until crisp. Pour off most of the fat and then add the chopped onions. Cook the onions until transparent.

3 Add the dried chili and Tabasco and stir through. Drain the kidney beans and add to the frying pan. Fold in the potatoes gently to avoid breaking up the slices. Pour the lemon juice over the potatoes and season with salt and pepper. Warm through and transfer to a serving dish. Sprinkle with chopped fresh herbs.

Serves 4

SILLISALATTI

I love the name of this Finnish salad — a combination of diced ingredients that turn red when the beets are mixed in. Serve it sprinkled with coarsely chopped fresh herbs. The contrast of red and green is beautifully summery.

Potatoes	4 large, boiled and peeled
Pickled beets	3
Marinated herring	1/2 lb (225 g), chopped
Apple	1, peeled and cored
Lemon juice	1 tsp (5 mL)
Spanish onion	1, peeled and thinly sliced
Vinaigrette dressing	3 Tbsp (50 mL)
Beet juice (from pickled beets)	2 Tbsp (25 mL)
Salt	1 tsp (5 mL)
Pepper	1/4 tsp (1 mL)
Fresh mixed herbs (e.g. dill, parsley, chives)	2 Tbsp (25 mL) coarsely chopped

1 Dice the potatoes and beets into even-sized pieces and combine with the chopped herring in a large salad bowl. Chop the apple and sprinkle it with lemon juice to prevent it from turning brown. Add it to the ingredients in the bowl, along with the onion rings.

2 Combine the vinaigrette and beet juice and pour it over the salad. Toss thoroughly and season with salt and pepper.

3 Serve topped with chopped herbs.

Serves 6

ALOO RAITA

Raita is an Indian yoghurt dish. This potato raita, with the crunchiness of cucumber, makes a refreshing accompaniment to meats and curries.

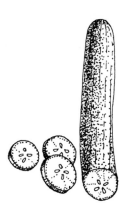

Potatoes	4, boiled, skinned and sliced
English cucumber	1 small, thinly sliced
Plain yoghurt	2 cups (500 mL)
Onion	1, peeled and finely chopped
Ground cumin	1/2 tsp (2 mL)
Chili powder	1/4 tsp (1 mL)
Pepper	1/4 tsp (1 mL)
Salt	1/2 tsp (2 mL)
Fresh parsley	1 Tbsp (15 mL) finely chopped
Fresh coriander, optional	1 tsp (5 mL) finely chopped

1 Combine all the ingredients and gently mix together.

2 Chill in the refrigerator for at least one hour before serving.

Serves 4

SHAKER SALAD

The Shakers of the east coast of the United States have a fine touch with food. They make it simple, yet interesting, and this is a good example of their special flair.

Potatoes	6 medium
Bacon	4 slices
Onion	1, peeled and finely chopped
Vinegar	3 Tbsp (50 mL)
Water	2 Tbsp (25 mL)
Salt	1 tsp (5 mL)
Sugar	1 tsp (5 mL)
Dry mustard	1 tsp (5 mL)
Fresh parsley	1 Tbsp (15 mL) finely chopped
Pepper	1 tsp (5 mL) coarsely cracked

1 Scrub the potatoes and boil them in their skins for 20 minutes or until cooked but still firm.

2 Cook the bacon in a frying pan until crisp. Remove the bacon and set aside on paper towels to absorb excess fat.

3 Pour off most of the bacon fat from the pan, leaving just enough to fry the chopped onions. Gently fry but do not brown the onions. Leave the onions in the frying pan.

4 Peel the potatoes while they are still hot and slice them into a serving dish. Keep warm.

5 Break up the crisp bacon into bits. Add the bacon to the frying pan containing the onions and combine with the vinegar, water, salt, sugar and mustard. Stir the contents and bring to a boil.

6 Pour the hot dressing over the potatoes and toss them to coat well. Garnish with chopped parsley and pepper.

Serves 4

CLARE'S SALAD

Whenever I make this salad, it disappears as fast as it hits the table; there are never any leftovers. My daughter, Clare, mastered this recipe when she was twelve and it's been her favourite contribution to every pot luck supper ever since.

Potatoes	6 medium
Eggs	4, hard-boiled
Mayonnaise	1 cup (250 mL)
Green onions	4, trimmed and chopped
Fresh parsley	1/2 cup (125 mL) finely chopped
Salt	1 tsp (5 mL)
Pepper	1/2 tsp (2 mL)

1 Scrub the potatoes and boil them in their skins for 20 minutes or until cooked but still firm. Drain the potatoes and run them under cold water to prevent further cooking.

2 Peel the eggs and chop them coarsely into a large mixing bowl. Add the mayonnaise, chopped green onions and parsley, salt and pepper.

3 Chop the potatoes coarsely into cubes, leaving the skins on. Add to the other ingredients in the bowl and mix thoroughly.

Serves 6

MAIN COURSES

A Day-long Romance with the Potato

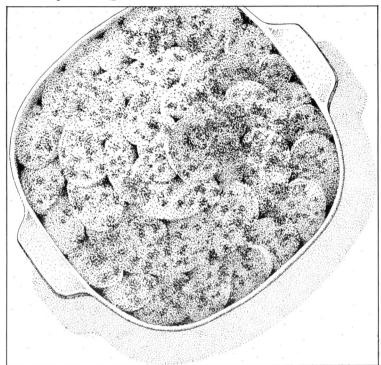

When Rick and I started testing recipes for this book, we were astonished that we could come up with such a range of main-course potato dishes. At first we made the mistake of thinking of potatoes mainly as a side dish; how wrong we were.

The breakfast recipes were the most fun for us because they gave our family a reason to get together on weekends to share a late but hearty breakfast. The opportunity to use up the leftover potatoes from the night before in various forms of hash or bubble and squeak was a challenge to our ingenuity, and it also gave everyone a chance to get in on the cooking.

Lunches were a pleasant surprise as well because, contrary to popular belief, there are many simple ways to prepare low-calorie, light potato dishes. Take, for example, the potato health loaf or the potato melt.

For dinner, curries, casseroles and croquettes were just the beginning. Although we're a relatively small family, with just four of us

55

living at home, we found we were buying 50-pound (23-kg) bags of potatoes every other week. Our book is now finished, but our potato habit is here to stay. Not long ago my daughter, Clare, called me at work wailing, ''Mom, there's no food in the house.'' I directed her to the bulging cupboards and refrigerator, but she said, ''No, I mean we're out of potatoes.'' This mother's heart was chastened and subdued by this obvious failure to provide for my family.

Main Courses

SUNSHINE POTATOES

When making this dish, try to get the freshest eggs possible. You will find that the fried egg white and yolk retain their shapes better if the eggs are very fresh. Sunshine potatoes served with ham and broiled tomatoes make a hearty winter brunch.

Butter	1 1/2 Tbsp (22.5 mL)
Onion	1 medium, peeled and finely chopped
Tomatoes	2 medium, peeled and seeded
Garlic	1 clove, minced
Fresh parsley	1 Tbsp (15 mL) finely chopped
Salt	1 tsp (5 mL)
Worcestershire sauce	1 tsp (5 mL)
Eggs	5, very fresh
Mashed potatoes	3 cups (750 mL)
Paprika	1/2 tsp (2 mL)

Preheat oven to 350°F (180°C).

1 Melt 1 Tbsp (15 mL) of the butter in a frying pan. When the foam subsides, fry the chopped onions for about 5 minutes or until transparent.

2 Coarsely chop the tomatoes and add to the onions. Fry over moderate heat for about 5 minutes to reduce the liquid in the tomatoes. Add the minced garlic, parsley, salt and Worcester-shire sauce. Stir through and continue to cook for 1 minute.

3 In a large mixing bowl, beat one of the eggs until it becomes a pale lemon colour. Add the mashed potatoes and the tomato mixture and combine well.

4 On a greased baking sheet, spoon the mixture into 4 round nests, making sure that the mixture is firmly packed. Melt the remaining 1/2 Tbsp (7.5 mL) of butter and brush each nest with a little melted butter.

5 Bake in a moderate oven for 20–25 minutes.

6 While the nests are baking, fry the remaining 4 eggs, keeping the whites as close to the yolks as possible.

7 Using a spatula, transfer the potato nests onto individual serv-ing plates. Lift one fried egg into the centre of each nest and sprinkle with paprika.

Serves 4

POTATO OMELETTE

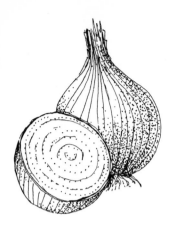

One of the great features of an omelette is that you can add almost anything to it. The slightly nutty flavour of the grated potatoes in this recipe gives the omelette a special touch.

Potatoes	3 medium
Bacon	2 strips, cut in small pieces
Onion	1, finely chopped
Eggs	4, beaten
Cream	2 Tbsp (25 mL)
Butter	2 Tbsp (25 mL), melted
Fresh chives or parsley	1 Tbsp (15 mL)
Pepper	1/2 tsp (2 mL)
Salt	1/2 tsp (2 mL)

1 Scrub the potatoes thoroughly but do not peel. Coarsely grate the unpeeled potatoes and squeeze out excess moisture.

2 Fry the bacon in a large, heavy frying pan. Drain off half the fat.

3 Add the chopped onions and fry until transparent. Add the grated potatoes, stir and cover. Cook over moderate heat for approximately 10 minutes.

4 In a separate bowl beat together the eggs and cream. Add the melted butter and seasonings and mix through.

5 Pour the mixture over the potatoes in the frying pan. Cook, uncovered, over low heat for approximately 8 minutes or until most of the egg mixture has set.

6 Finish off the omelette under the broiler for several minutes to set and lightly brown the top.

Serves 4

OVEN-BAKED POTATO OMELETTE

There are, not surprisingly, a number of versions of potato omelette. This baked omelette, using raw potatoes, is a traditional recipe from Finland.

Butter	2 Tbsp (25 mL)
Potatoes	3 medium, peeled
Eggs	3, beaten
Ground allspice, optional	1/4 tsp (1 mL)
Fresh dill	1 tsp (5 mL) finely chopped
Salt	1/2 tsp (2 mL)
Flour	1 Tbsp (15 mL)
Milk	1/2 cup (125 mL)

Preheat oven to 350°F (180°C).

1 Melt the butter and spread it over the bottom and sides of a fairly shallow oven-proof dish.

2 Grate the potatoes into a mixing bowl. Add the beaten eggs, allspice, dill and salt. Blend the flour into the milk and press out any lumps to make a smooth paste. Add the paste to the potato mixture, blending all the ingredients thoroughly.

3 Pour the mixture into the oven-proof dish. Bake at 350°F (180°C) for about 45 minutes or until the eggs have set.

Serves 4

ANCHOVY FRITTATA

This is really an omelette Italian style. Frittata, made with whatever fresh vegetables took our fancy, was the mainstay of our diet when we were staying in central Italy. The edible, warm yellow blossoms from zucchini (courgettes) make an intriguing addition to the colour and texture of this frittata.

Butter	2 Tbsp (25 mL)
Onion	1 medium, peeled and thinly sliced
Potato	1 large, peeled
Anchovy fillets	1 can, 2-oz (57-g)
Eggs	3, separated
Cream	1/2 cup (125 mL)
Salt	1/2 tsp (2 mL)
Pepper	1/4 tsp (1 mL)
Fresh parsley	1 Tbsp (15 mL) finely chopped
Zucchini (courgette) blossoms, optional	10 blossoms

Preheat oven to 375°F (190°C).

1 Melt the butter in a small saucepan. When the foam subsides, fry the sliced onions gently for about 5 minutes.

2 Slice the potato into thin rounds. Grease an oven-proof dish and spread the potato slices in a layer across the bottom of the dish. If you have enough, form a second layer of potatoes.

3 Spread the lightly fried onions on top of the potatoes in the dish.

4 Drain off and set aside the oil from the anchovies and chop the fillets into small pieces. Scatter the chopped anchovies on top of the onions. Cover the dish with a lid or aluminum foil and bake for 25 minutes at 375°F (190°C).

5 While the potatoes are baking, beat the egg yolks in a small bowl, then beat in the cream, salt and pepper and a little of the oil drained from the anchovies.

6 In another clean bowl beat the egg whites until foamy but not too dry. Gently fold them into the yolk mixture and add the chopped parsley.

7 If you are using zucchini blossoms, prepare them by removing the stems and pollen-coated centres (pistils). Wash them in cold water, drain and chop coarsely. Add to the egg mixture.

8 Remove the dish from the oven after 25 minutes and pour the egg and cream mixture over the contents. Reduce the oven heat to 350°F (180°C) and return the dish, uncovered, to the oven for another 25 minutes or until the eggs have set. Serve immediately.

Serves 4

POTATO SOUFFLÉ

Contrary to popular belief, a soufflé is a simple dish. Once you master the art of making it, it will become your reliable stand-by for emergencies. As long as you have at least four eggs, you can combine them with a variety of ingredients to produce either a sweet or savoury soufflé.

The basic rules go something like this:
Always preheat the oven.
Have the eggs at room temperature.
Separate the eggs and beat the whites until they are stiff but still moist.
Fold one-half of the beaten whites into the base mixture first, then lightly fold in the rest of the whites.
Do not open the oven door during the first 20 minutes of cooking.

Preheat oven to 375°F (190°C).

Eggs	4, yolks and whites separated*
Cream	1/2 cup (125 mL)
Butter	3 Tbsp (50 mL) melted
Salt	1/2 tsp (2 mL)
Pepper	1/4 tsp (1 mL)
Fresh chives	1 Tbsp (15 mL) finely chopped
Cheddar cheese	1/2 cup (125 mL) grated
Nutmeg	1/4 tsp (1 mL) freshly grated
Mashed potatoes	2 cups (500 mL)

* For extra height, add another egg white.

1 Grease a 9-inch (23-cm) soufflé dish or deep-sided casserole dish.

2 In a large mixing bowl beat the egg yolks until they are a lemon colour. Beat in the cream, melted butter, salt, pepper, chives, cheese and nutmeg. Add the mashed potatoes and combine thoroughly.

3 In a second bowl, beat the egg whites until they are stiff but still moist. Be sure to use a clean fork or egg beater.

4 Fold in half the egg whites, gently distributing the foam through the potato mixture. Lightly fold in the remaining whites.

5 Quickly spoon the mixture into the soufflé dish. Bake in a preheated oven at 375°F (190°C) for about 35 minutes, until it has risen and become golden brown. Serve at once.

Serves 4

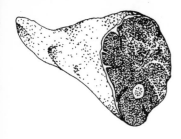

MEAT AND POTATO HASH

Hash is a mainstay of any cooking repertoire; it's based on the creative use of leftovers. Anyone who cooks a lot of potatoes knows enough to make extras for leftovers. Any kind of meat may be used, but corned beef, lamb or pork is best for a good, hearty hash.

Bacon	4 slices
Potatoes	6 medium, cooked
Leftover meat	2 cups (500 mL) chopped
Fresh parsley	1 Tbsp (15 mL) finely chopped
Salt	1/2 tsp (2 mL)
Pepper	1/4 tsp (1 mL)
Cayenne, optional	1/4 tsp (1 mL)
Eggs	2, beaten

1 In a large, heavy frying pan fry the bacon strips. When they are cooked, chop them and set aside.

2 Cut the potatoes into small dice. Combine with the chopped meat, parsley, salt, pepper and cayenne.

3 Drain the excess bacon fat from the frying pan, leaving just enough to fry the potatoes and meat. Add the potato and meat mixture. Stir well and cook over moderate heat until the potatoes begin to brown. Add the chopped bacon.

4 After about 15 minutes, when the ingredients in the pan have browned, add the beaten eggs. Do not stir after you add the egg mixture but allow the egg to set. Serve hot.

A hearty breakfast for 4

Variation: OVEN-BAKED HASH

To the ingredients in the preceding recipe add 1 cup (250 mL) of stock or milk. Place all the ingredients in a greased casserole dish, placing two extra strips of bacon on the bottom and two strips on the top.

Bake at 375°F (190°C) for 35 minutes.

BUBBLE AND SQUEAK

Bubble and squeak gets its name from the sound emitted by the potatoes, cabbage and onion sizzling in the pan. It's not authentic if the mixture does not have a crust on the bottom, so you will need a heavy frying pan — one that distributes the heat evenly. Some people like the crust only on the bottom, while others prefer to turn over the mixture to produce as much crust as possible. Leftover colcannon is especially good as a base for bubble and squeak. (See the recipe for colcannon elsewhere in this chapter.)

Bacon	4 strips
Onion	1 medium, peeled and thinly sliced
Cabbage	1 cup (250 mL) chopped
Mashed potatoes	2 cups (500 mL) or equal amount of leftover colcannon
Sweet potato or yam	1, peeled, cooked and mashed
Peas	1/2 cup (125 mL), cooked
Salt and pepper	to taste

1 In a large, heavy frying pan fry the bacon strips until crisp. Set aside the bacon and pour off the excess fat. Reserve the fat. Fry the onion slices in the pan for about 7 minutes or until soft and slightly browned. Add the cabbage and fry until soft but still green.

2 Combine the remaining ingredients and add to the pan. (If you are using leftover colcannon as a base, you may not need to use any additional salt and pepper.) Stir fry until browned and warmed through. Allow the mixture to become slightly crusty; this might take about 20 minutes. If the mixture becomes too dry, add a little of the reserved bacon fat.

3 Transfer to a warm serving dish and garnish with the bacon strips.

Serves 4

COLCANNON

Both Scotland and Ireland have versions of colcannon. In some communities, there is also a tradition of hiding small charms in the mixture. The finder is blessed with good fortune and an extra serving of colcannon.

Colcannon makes a grand foundation for bubble and squeak. (A recipe for bubble and squeak appears elsewhere in this chapter.) Make plenty so that there will be leftovers for breakfast.

Potatoes	6 large, unpeeled
Parsnips	2, peeled and coarsely chopped
Leeks	2
Milk or cream	2/3 cup (150 mL)
Butter	2 Tbsp (25 mL)
Cabbage	1 large wedge, shredded
Fresh parsley	1 Tbsp (15 mL) finely chopped
Salt	1 tsp (5 mL)
Pepper	1/2 tsp (2 mL)

1 Cut the potatoes into large pieces of approximately equal size. Place the potatoes in a pot of salted water, bring to a boil, then reduce the heat to a simmer. Unless the pieces are very large, the potatoes should be cooked in 20 minutes. If a fork penetrates easily, the potatoes are done. Drain and peel.

2 Put the parsnips in a pot of cold water and bring to a boil. Add a sprinkling of sugar to the water, if you wish. Boil, uncovered, for a few minutes, then cover and simmer for about 20 minutes or until tender. Drain well.

3 Trim off the rough, green sections of the leeks, retaining only the white interior leaves and the tenderest green parts. Cut off the root. With a sharp knife, slice the leeks in half lengthwise to expose the inner leaves. Hold under running water and separate the leaves to wash out all the grit that clings to them. Chop the leeks coarsely.

4 Sweat the leeks for about 20 minutes in the milk or cream and 1 Tbsp (15 mL) of the butter.

5 Steam the cabbage for approximately 7 minutes until soft but still green. Drain well.

6 Mash together the potatoes and parsnip. Add the leeks and cream and blend well. Mix in the drained cabbage, parsley, salt and pepper.

7 Spoon into a warm serving dish. Make a well in the centre and add an extra dab of butter.

Serves 6, or 4 if you want leftovers for bubble and squeak.

Top Left: Ilmi's Potato Bread (see page 150)
Top Right: Johnny Cakes and Latkes (see pages 145 & 147)
Bottom: Aussie Chowder (see page 31)

SCANDINAVIAN HASH

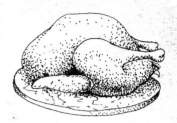

Hash and bubble and squeak are cousins. Both are ideal for using up leftovers, particularly around Christmas when there's plenty of leftover meat and, usually, extra mouths to feed at breakfast. Hash makes a hearty breakfast, with or without eggs.

Butter	2 Tbsp (25 mL)
Onion	1 large, peeled and finely chopped
Potatoes	6, cooked, peeled and diced
Cooked meat (ham, pork, or turkey)	1 cup (250 mL) diced
Green onions	2, finely chopped
Fresh dill	2 Tbsp (25 mL) finely chopped
Salt	1 tsp (5 mL)
Pepper	1/2 tsp (2 mL)

1 Melt the butter in a large frying pan. Fry the chopped onions gently for about 5 minutes or until they become transparent.

2 Add all the remaining ingredients and fry over moderate heat until browned. Turn over frequently with a spatula, but try not to break up the potatoes too much.

3 Top each serving with a fried or poached egg, if you like.

Serves 4

POTATO CROQUETTES

Eggs	3
Mashed potatoes	2 cups (500 mL)
Salt	1 tsp (5 mL)
Fresh parsley	1 Tbsp (15 mL) finely chopped
Milk	2 Tbsp (25 mL)
Dry breadcrumbs	1 cup (250 mL)
Butter	1 Tbsp (15 mL)
Oil	2 Tbsp (25 mL)

1 In a large mixing bowl beat two of the eggs. Mix in the mashed potatoes, salt and parsley. Add the milk and combine thoroughly. Form the mixture into small cigar shapes about 2 inches (5 cm) long. Refrigerate for about 30 minutes.

2 Mix the remaining egg with a little water and beat well to make an egg-wash to coat the croquettes.

3 Spread the breadcrumbs on a dinner plate.

4 Dip each croquette into the egg-wash and coat well; then roll it in the breadcrumbs. Set aside on a plate until all the croquettes have been coated. Repeat the coating to give each croquette a firm seal.

5 Heat the butter and oil in a large frying pan over moderate heat. The butter and oil should be hot enough to make the croquettes sizzle when they are placed in the pan. Fry the croquettes, browning them on all sides, for about 7 minutes.

Makes 6 croquettes

POTATO AND CHICKEN CROQUETTES

Eggs	3
Cooked chicken	1 cup (250 mL) finely diced or minced
Mashed potatoes	2 cups (500 mL)
Garlic	1 clove, minced
Dried sage	1/2 tsp (2 mL)
Salt	1/2 tsp (2 mL)
Dry breadcrumbs	1 cup (250 mL)
Oil	for deep frying

1 In a large mixing bowl beat two of the eggs. Add the minced chicken, mashed potatoes, minced garlic, sage and salt. Mix thoroughly and divide the mixture into eight equal portions. Form into cigar shapes about 2 inches (5 cm) long. Refrigerate for about 30 minutes.

2 In another bowl mix the remaining egg with a little water and beat well to make an egg-wash to coat the croquettes.

3 Spread the breadcrumbs on a dinner plate.

4 Dip each croquette into the egg-wash and coat well; then roll it in breadcrumbs. Set aside on a plate until all the croquettes have been coated. Repeat the coating to give each croquette a firm seal.

5 Heat the oil to 375°F (190°C). Deep fry the croquettes, a few at a time, until golden. They will rise to the surface when they are cooked. This should take about 3 minutes. Drain well on paper towels.

Makes 8 croquettes

IRISH STEW

The fates of the Irish and the potato are as tightly intertwined as the thorny vines of the Irish roses that decorate the Book of Kells. Where would the Irish be without the potato? Where would the potato be without the Irish? Potatoes have sustained the Irish nation for some 300 years, and you'd be unlikely to find a table that didn't offer a steaming bowl of potatoes to all comers. But perhaps because potatoes are so dear to the Irish heart, they are generally eaten plain. Irish cooks don't have a long repertoire of fancy ways to cook potatoes. They boil them or mash them or put them in stews such as this one, but on the whole, the Irish take their potatoes, like their Guinness, straight.

Stewing lamb	2 lb (900 g)
Bouquet garni	1 sachet
Celery	1 stalk including leaves
Salt	1/2 tsp (2 mL)
Pepper	1/2 tsp (2 mL)
Onions	3 medium
Potatoes	6 large
Fresh parsley	1 Tbsp (15 mL) finely chopped

1 Trim off the fat and cut the meat into even-sized pieces. Put the meat into a large pot, add enough water to cover and bring to a boil. Skim off the foam on the surface. Add the bouquet garni, the stalk of celery, salt and pepper. Peel and cut one onion into quarters and add to the meat. Simmer gently for 1/2 hour, skimming off the foam on top from time to time.

2 Peel the potatoes and cut into chunks of even size. Peel and chop the remaining onions. When the meat has simmered for 1/2 hour, add the potatoes and onions and continue to cook for another 1/2 hour. Check the seasoning and adjust to taste.

3 Remove the celery and bouquet garni. Skim off any fat from the surface of the stew. Add the chopped parsley and serve.

Serves 4-6

JOYCE'S LAYERED POTATOES

This recipe, along with several other Hungarian recipes that appear in this book, was given to me by my friend Joyce. For a few pleasant months last summer, Joyce worked at CJRT in Toronto, and each evening, when our work was finished, we sat as women have for centuries, talking about food and families. Joyce's approach to cooking gave me an incentive to try new food combinations, and her down-to-earth wisdom on parenting helped me through some anxious times.

Potatoes	6, boiled in their skins
Onion	1 medium
Oil	1 Tbsp (15 mL)
Sour cream	1 cup (250 mL)
Whipping cream	1/2 cup (125 mL)
Salt	1 tsp (5 mL)
Pepper	1/4 tsp (1 mL)
Eggs	4, hard-boiled
Cooked ham	1 cup (250 mL) diced
Butter	2 Tbsp (25 mL) melted
Dry breadcrumbs	1 cup (250 mL)

Preheat oven to 350°F (180°C).

1 Peel the cooked potatoes and cut into 1/4-inch (6-mm) slices.

2 Thinly slice the onion and fry in a little oil, just until soft.

3 Combine the sour cream and whipping cream in a mixing bowl.

4 Grease an oven-proof casserole dish and arrange one-third of the potato slices across the bottom. Season with a little salt and pepper. Lightly spread the sliced onions on top of the potatoes. Cover with a little of the cream mixture.

5 Peel and slice the hard-boiled eggs and place on top of the onions. Add another layer of potatoes, season with salt and pepper, then add a little more of the cream mixture. Sprinkle with the diced ham and pour the remaining cream mixture over it. Top with a final layer of potatoes.

6 Toss the breadcrumbs in the melted butter and sprinkle over the potatoes.

7 Bake in a moderate oven for 30–35 minutes or until the top is brown and bubbly.

Serves 4

POTATO PIE

A pie usually involves pastry, but in this case, the term is used rather loosely. This recipe combines all the ingredients in one dish and makes a satisfying main course meal.

You'll need an oven-proof dish, approximately 9 inches (23 cm) in diameter.

Leeks	2
Butter	1 Tbsp (15 mL)
Potatoes	6, medium, cooked and mashed
Cheddar cheese	2 cups (500 mL) grated
Fresh mixed herbs (parsley, chives)*	1 Tbsp (15 mL) finely chopped
Dry mustard	1 tsp (5 mL)
Salt	1/4 tsp (1 mL)
Pepper	a pinch
Dry breadcrumbs	3 Tbsp (50 mL)
Egg	1, hard-boiled

* include watercress, if available.

White Sauce

Butter	2 Tbsp (25 mL)
All-purpose flour	1 Tbsp (15 mL) sifted
Milk	1 cup (250 mL)
Cider	1/2 cup (125 mL)

Preheat oven to 375°F (190°C).

1 Trim off the rough, green sections of the leeks, retaining only the white interior leaves and the tenderest green parts. Cut off the root. With a sharp knife, slice the leeks in half lengthwise to expose the inner leaves. Hold under running water and separate the leaves to remove all the grit that clings to them. Chop the leeks coarsely.

2 Melt the butter in a frying pan. Add the leeks and sweat them until soft, about 15 minutes.

3 Combine the mashed potatoes, leeks, grated cheese, herbs, mustard, salt and pepper. Spoon the mixture into a pie dish which has been greased and lightly sprinkled with bread-crumbs. Reserve some breadcrumbs for use as a topping.

4 To make the sauce, melt the butter in a saucepan, then remove the saucepan from the heat. Add the flour to the butter and mix well with a wooden spoon. Return to the heat and cook over moderate heat until the mixture begins to foam. Remove the pot from the heat. Gradually add the milk, and with a wooden

spoon mix well to prevent lumps. Return the pot to low heat and stir until the mixture thickens. Cook gently for two more minutes. Add the cider and mix in thoroughly.

5 Pour the sauce over the potato mixture. Sprinkle the top with the remaining breadcrumbs and dot with extra butter.

6 Bake at 375°F (190°C) for 30 minutes or until firm and golden on top.

7 Finely chop the hard-boiled egg and sprinkle over top of the pie.

Serves 6

POTATO GOULASH

One of the potato's finest virtues is that it absorbs flavours, particularly the pungent flavours of spices. That's why potatoes make such good curries and stews. Try this hearty Hungarian potato stew; it tastes even better if you make it a day ahead.

Butter	2 Tbsp (25 mL)
Onions	2 medium, peeled and chopped
Potatoes	6 large, peeled and sliced
Sweet paprika	1 Tbsp (15 mL)
Garlic	1 clove, minced
Dried marjoram	1 tsp (5 mL)
Caraway seeds, optional	1 tsp (5 mL)
Salt	1 tsp (5 mL)
Pepper	1 tsp (5 mL)
Chicken stock	1 cup (250 mL)
Sour cream	1/3 cup (75 mL)
Fresh parsley	1 Tbsp (15 mL) finely chopped

1 Melt the butter in a large frying pan. When the foam subsides, add the onions and fry them for about 7 minutes.

2 Add the potatoes and toss the slices to coat them thoroughly with butter.

3 Add the paprika and garlic and fry gently for about 3 minutes. Add the marjoram, caraway seeds, salt and pepper. Pour in the chicken stock.

4 Cover the frying pan with a lid or aluminum foil and cook over low heat for about 20 minutes.

5 Serve topped with sour cream and chopped parsley.

Serves 4

ALOO GOBI WITH FRIED ONIONS

This is a very popular Indian vegetable curry made with cauliflower and potato. The spices included in this recipe will make a curry mixture; however, if you prefer to substitute prepared curry powder, do so by all means.

Onion	2, peeled and sliced
Ghee (clarified butter) or oil	4 Tbsp (60 mL)
Potatoes	6, scrubbed and parboiled
Cauliflower	1/2 head, cut into florets
Ground turmeric	1/2 tsp (2 mL)
Ground cumin	1/2 tsp (2 mL)
Chili powder	1/4 tsp (1 mL)
Salt	1 tsp (5 mL)
Sugar	1/4 tsp (1 mL)
Garam masala	1/2 tsp (2 mL)
Whole tomatoes	1 can, 19-oz (540-mL)
Chicken stock	1 1/2 cups (375 mL)
Garlic	2 cloves, minced
Plain yoghurt	1 cup (250 mL)
Fresh parsley	1 Tbsp (15 mL) finely chopped
Fresh coriander, optional	1 tsp (5 mL) finely chopped

1 In a large frying pan, fry the onions in 1 Tbsp (15 mL) of the ghee until they are quite brown but not burnt. Set aside.

2 Cut the parboiled potatoes into small chunks. Add 2 Tbsp (30 mL) of the ghee to the pan and fry the potatoes, a little at a time, until they are all lightly browned. Remove the potatoes and set aside. Add another Tbsp (15 mL) of ghee to the pan.

3 Add the cauliflower and fry until lightly browned. Remove the cauliflower and set aside with the potatoes.

4 Add the turmeric, cumin, chili powder, salt, sugar and garam masala to the pan and mix them together. Cook gently for about 1 minute. Add the can of whole tomatoes, including the juice. Stir well, breaking up the tomatoes. Fry gently for about 2 minutes. Add a little chicken stock and bring to a boil. Use the remaining chicken stock if the vegetables seem to be boiling dry or if you prefer more sauce.

5 Add the potato chunks and minced garlic, cover and cook gently for about 15 minutes. Add the cauliflower, cover and cook for about 10 minutes or until the cauliflower is tender.

6 Transfer to a warm serving dish and top with yoghurt, fried onions, chopped parsley and coriander.

Serves 4

POTATO KEDGEREE

This is an Anglo-Indian dish which we have further Anglicized with the substitution of potatoes for rice. A kedgeree is usually a combination of eggs, fish and rice, bound together by a creamy sauce.

Potatoes	5 medium, boiled in their skins
Butter	2 Tbsp (25 mL)
Onion	1, peeled and finely chopped
Mild curry powder	2 tsp (10 mL)
Zucchini (courgette)	1, sliced
Eggs	4, hard-boiled
Peas	1 cup (250 mL), cooked
Plain yoghurt	1 cup (250 mL)
Lemon juice	1 tsp (5 mL)
Grated lemon peel*	1/4 tsp (1 mL)
Salt	1 tsp (5 mL)
Pepper	1/2 tsp (2 mL)
Fresh mint or watercress	a few sprigs for garnish

*With a fine grater remove just the yellow surface of the skin of a lemon. This will give you a fresh, concentrated lemon flavour from the oils and fibre on the surface, without the bitterness of the white membrane underneath.

1 Peel the cooked potatoes and chop coarsely.

2 Melt the butter in a large frying pan. When the foam subsides, add the chopped onions and curry powder and fry gently for about 5 minutes.

3 Add the chopped potatoes and fry for another 5 minutes, stirring to combine. Stir in the sliced zucchini and continue cooking for 5 minutes.

4 Peel the eggs and cut into halves. Add the eggs, peas, yoghurt, lemon juice, grated lemon peel, salt and pepper to the pan. Combine carefully so that the ingredients are not mashed together. Heat through but do not overcook.

5 Transfer to a serving dish and garnish with sprigs of mint or watercress.

Serves 4

CHICKEN PARMENTIER

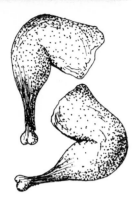

Antoine-Auguste Parmentier owed his life to the potatoes that sustained him through a long stay in a prison in Germany. Curious about them and no doubt grateful to them as well, he championed their cause in the court of Louis XVI. In French cuisine the word Parmentier indicates that the potato is an important ingredient.

Oil	2 Tbsp (30 mL)
Chicken legs	8
Potatoes	4 large
Butter	2 Tbsp (30 mL)
White wine	1/2 cup (125 mL)
Cayenne	1/4 tsp (1 mL)
Salt	1/2 tsp (2 mL)
Fresh parsley	1 Tbsp (15 mL) finely chopped

1 Coat a large frying pan with 1 Tbsp (15 mL) of the oil. Fry the chicken legs in the oil until cooked and golden on all sides. This should take about 20 minutes.

2 Peel and dice the potatoes and soak them in cold water for about 5 minutes. Drain them well and dry with a clean tea towel or paper towels.

3 While the chicken is cooking, melt the butter in another frying pan and add the remaining 1 Tbsp (15 mL) of oil. When the fat is hot, add the diced potatoes and fry them over medium heat, turning them over to brown on all sides. This should take 10–15 minutes.

4 When the chicken is cooked, remove the pieces from the pan and set aside on a warm platter. Pour off the excess oil from the pan and add the wine. Mix it well with the sediment in the pan and cook gently until the wine has been reduced by half. Season with salt and cayenne.

5 Spoon the potatoes into a serving dish, making a well in the centre. Arrange the chicken legs in the centre and pour the wine from the pan over the chicken. Sprinkle with finely chopped parsley.

Serves 4

POTATO AND TOFU STIR-FRY

For an interesting light lunch try this unusual combination of tofu, crunchy water chestnuts and smooth, firm potatoes. Top it off with the peppery zing of watercress and a dash of tamari sauce.

Peanut oil	2 Tbsp (25 mL)
Onion	1 medium, peeled and sliced
Potatoes	4 large, boiled and diced
Tofu (bean curd)	2 squares
Water chestnuts	1 can, 10-oz (284-mL), drained and sliced
Pepper	1/4 tsp (1 mL)
Tamari sauce or soy sauce	1 tsp (5 mL)
Watercress	1 Tbsp (15 mL) finely chopped
Fresh dill	1 tsp (5 mL)

1 Heat the oil in a wok and fry the sliced onions until lightly golden.

2 Add the cooked potatoes and stir fry until lightly browned.

3 Drain the tofu and carefully pat dry with a clean tea towel. Cut into 12 pieces.

4 Add the tofu pieces and sliced water chestnuts and fry for about 3 minutes. Season with pepper and tamari sauce and stir through.

5 Serve topped with chopped watercress and dill.

Serves 4

POTATO MELT

I usually don't like recipes that mix lots of ingredients together, but this dish is an exception. Not only is there an interesting combination of textures — crunchy and tender — but there is an attractive mixture of strong colours.

New potatoes	12, washed
Butter	1 Tbsp (15 mL)
Onion	1, peeled and sliced
Salt	1 tsp (5 mL)
Broccoli	1 head, including stem
Sweet red pepper	1/2 a pepper, cored
Oil	1 Tbsp (15 mL)
Cauliflower	12 florets
Mung bean sprouts	1 1/2 cups (375 mL)
Fresh mixed herbs (parsley, chives)	1 Tbsp (15 mL)
Sharp Cheddar cheese	1 cup (250 mL) grated

1 Cook the unpeeled potatoes in boiling water for about 10 minutes or until cooked but still firm. Drain and cut the potatoes into halves.

2 Melt the butter in a wok and fry the sliced onions until lightly browned. Add the potatoes and brown them a little. Season with salt.

3 Transfer the potatoes and onions to a large serving dish that will withstand the heat of the broiler for a short time. If you don't have such a dish, use a frying pan. Keep the dish warm.

4 Trim off the hard, lower part of the broccoli stem. Slice the stem and separate the florets and small stalks.

5 Slice the red pepper into strips about 1 inch long (2.5 cm).

6 Heat the oil in the wok. Fry the cauliflower florets for about 3 minutes. Add the red pepper and broccoli and stir fry for another 3 to 5 minutes. The vegetables should be partially cooked but still crisp.

7 Add the stir-fried vegetables to the potatoes. Mix in the mung bean sprouts and finely chopped herbs.

8 Top with a layer of grated cheese and broil until the cheese has melted. Serve immediately.

Serves 4

FINNISH MEAT BALLS

There was always something distinctive about food made by Rick's Finnish grandmother. Although she lived in northern Canada for more than sixty years, her touch included a little extra Finnish magic that evoked memories of childhood for Rick. After she died, we tried to reproduce our favourites from the few sketchy recipes she left us. I think this one does her justice.

Mashed potatoes	1 cup (250 mL)
Ground pork	1 lb (450 g)
Eggs	2, beaten
Ground allspice	1/2 tsp (2 mL)
Salt	1 tsp (5 mL)
Onion	1, peeled and grated
Fresh dill	1 Tbsp (15 mL) finely chopped, plus sprigs for garnish
Potato or all-purpose flour	3 Tbsp (50 mL)
Butter	1 Tbsp (15 mL)
Oil	1 Tbsp (15 mL)
Sour cream	1 cup (250 mL)

Preheat oven to 375°F (190°C).

1 In a large mixing bowl combine the potatoes, pork, beaten eggs, allspice, salt, grated onion and dill.

2 With floured hands, shape the mixture into balls about 1 inch (2.5 cm) in diameter. As the balls are shaped, set them out on a large plate. Once all the mixture has been shaped, sprinkle a little flour on the meat balls and rest them in the refrigerator for about half an hour.

3 Heat the butter and oil in a large frying pan. Fry the meat balls gently until browned on all sides. Arrange in an oven-proof serving dish, top with sour cream and place in a moderate oven (375°F, 190°C) for 10 minutes. Serve garnished with sprigs of fresh dill.

Serves 4

FISH AND POTATO CASSEROLE

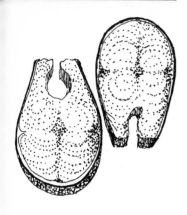

The creaminess of the fish and potatoes go well together. Some may think the flavours are bland, but the gentle, soothing taste and texture of this casserole are satisfying. It's a fine dish for Sunday suppers or lunches.

Potatoes	4 medium
Onion	1 medium
Butter	2 Tbsp (25 mL)
Halibut or cod	1 lb (450 g) filleted
Eggs	2
Milk	2 cups (500 mL)
Ground allspice	1/2 tsp (2 mL)
Salt	1/2 tsp (2 mL)
Pepper	1/4 tsp (1 mL)
Fresh dill	1 tsp (5 mL) finely chopped
Dry breadcrumbs	1/2 cup (125 mL)
Lemon wedges	for garnish

Preheat oven to 375°F (190°C).

1 Peel the potatoes and slice thinly. Peel the onion and also slice thinly. Melt the butter in a large, heavy frying pan and sauté the sliced onions for about 5 minutes. Remove the onions and set aside. Sauté the potatoes for about 5 minutes.

2 Grease an oven-proof casserole dish and arrange a layer of potatoes on the bottom. Cover with a layer of fish and top with a layer of onions.

3 Beat the eggs and mix well with the milk, allspice, salt and pepper. Pour the mixture over the layers in the casserole dish. Sprinkle with dill and breadcrumbs. Dot with extra butter.

4 Bake at 375°F (190°C) for 1 hour. Garnish with lemon wedges and serve hot.

Serves 4

ITALIAN POTATOES

Italy is not a country that springs to mind when potatoes are mentioned; Italians have their pasta and breads to provide starch. But in this dish the potatoes absorb fragrance from the oregano and parsley and a heady saltiness from the anchovies. It's enough to convert even the most ardent pasta eater.

For this recipe you'll need a deep-sided pie dish approximately 9 inches (23 cm) in diameter.

Potatoes	6 medium, cooked and mashed
Butter	2 Tbsp (30 mL)
Garlic	1 clove, crushed
Sour cream	1/2 cup (125 mL)
Fresh parsley	1 Tbsp (15 mL) finely chopped
Dried oregano	1 tsp (5 mL)
Salt	1/4 tsp (1 mL)
Freshly ground pepper	a pinch
Dry breadcrumbs	1 cup (250 mL)
Mozzarella cheese	1 cup (250 mL) grated
Anchovy fillets	1 can, 2-oz (57-g), drained

Preheat oven to 350°F (180°C).

1 Combine the mashed potatoes, 1 Tbsp (15 mL) of the butter, crushed garlic, sour cream, parsley, oregano, salt and pepper. Spoon the mixture into a pie dish that has been greased and lightly sprinkled with breadcrumbs.

2 Top with a layer of Mozzarella cheese. Sprinkle on a layer of breadcrumbs. Dot with the remaining 1 Tbsp (15 mL) of butter.

3 Bake for 20 minutes in a moderate oven 350°F (180°C).

4 Remove from the oven and top with strips of anchovies, arranged in a lattice pattern. Return to the oven for 5 minutes. Serve hot.

Serves 6

POTATO AND SAUSAGE CASEROLE

If you can't find small cocktail sausages, use ordinary sausages and slice them into chunks.

Potatoes	6 medium
Cocktail sausages	1 lb (450 g)
Onions	2 medium, peeled and sliced
Apples	2, peeled, cored and sliced
Flour	1 Tbsp (15 mL)
Fresh dill, optional	1 Tbsp (15 mL) finely chopped
Salt	1 tsp (5 mL)
Pepper	1/2 tsp (2 mL)
Sour cream	1/2 cup (125 mL)
Chicken stock	1 cup (250 mL)

Preheat oven to 350°F (180°C).

1 Boil the potatoes in their skins until tender (about 20 minutes). Peel the potatoes and chop them coarsely.

2 Fry the sausages gently in a large frying pan. Pour off most of the fat and set the sausages aside and keep warm.

3 Add the onions to the frying pan and cook them for about 5 minutes, then add the apple slices. Fry gently for a few minutes to soften the apples.

4 Combine the flour, salt, pepper and chopped dill and dredge the potatoes and sausages separately in the seasoned flour.

5 Stir the sour cream into the apple and onion mixture in the pan.

6 In an oven-proof dish alternate layers of potato, sour cream mixture and sausages. Pour the chicken stock onto the mixture.

7 Cover with a lid or aluminum foil and bake at 350°F (180°C) for 35 minutes.

Serves 4

POTATO AND TUNA BAKE

This is an ideal supper for Sunday evenings after skating or skiing. It can be made ahead and reheated quickly in the oven.

Potatoes	5 large, peeled and diced
Onion	2 large, peeled and minced
Butter	3 Tbsp (50 mL)
Garlic	1 clove, minced
Salt	1/2 tsp (2 mL)
Pepper	1/4 tsp (1 mL)
Tuna	1 can, 6.5-oz (184-g)
Eggs	3, beaten
Cream	1 cup (250 mL)
Swiss cheese	1/2 cup (125 mL) grated

Preheat oven to 375°F (190°C).

1 Boil the diced potatoes in salted water for about 8 minutes. Drain well.

2 While the potatoes are cooking, gently sweat the onions in 2 Tbsp (25 mL) of the butter until soft but not browned. Add the minced garlic, salt and pepper.

3 Spread half of the diced potatoes in the bottom of a greased casserole dish. Top with a layer of the onion mixture.

4 Drain the can of tuna and reserve the liquid. Break up the pieces of tuna and spread the flakes over the onion in the casserole dish. Top with the remaining potatoes.

5 Beat together the eggs, cream and liquid from the tuna. Pour the mixture over the potatoes, shaking the dish gently to distribute the liquid through the layers.

6 Sprinkle the grated cheese on top and dot with a few dabs of butter.

7 Bake in the oven at 375°F (190°C) for approximately 40 minutes.

Serves 4-6

DUTCH APPLE AND POTATO SUPPER

This combination may not seem so surprising when you know that the Dutch word for potato is *aardappel* or earth apple. The tart flavour of the apple goes well with the mashed potatoes, and the bacon adds a contrasting texture as well as an interesting flavour.

Cooking apples	6
Potatoes	6, peeled and cut in chunks
Water	2 cups
Salt	2 tsp (10 mL)
Side bacon	12 strips
Butter	2 Tbsp (25 mL)
Pepper	1/2 tsp (2 mL)
Lemon juice	2 tsp (10 mL)

1 Peel the apples and cut them into quarters. Cut out the cores and sprinkle the apples with lemon juice to keep them from darkening.

2 Combine the apples and potatoes in a large saucepan with the water and 1 tsp (5 mL) of the salt. Bring to a boil and cover with a tight-fitting lid. Lower the heat and cook gently for 30 minutes.

3 Meanwhile fry the bacon until just crisp. Set the bacon aside and reserve a little of the dripping. Keep the bacon warm.

4 When the potatoes and apples are cooked, drain them well. Mash them together with butter, salt and pepper and a small amount of the bacon dripping.

5 Transfer the potato mixture to a warm serving dish and top with the bacon strips.

Serves 4

POTATO AND FISH MURAT

This is an unusual combination of textures and flavours. The cucumbers add a freshness to the delicate flavour of the fish.

Flounder or sole	1 lb (450 g) fillets
Potatoes	4 large
Oil	1 1/2 Tbsp (22.5 mL)
Salt	2 tsp (10 mL)
Mushrooms	10 caps, washed
English cucumber	1 large, peeled and diced
Flour	2 Tbsp (25 mL)
Butter	2 Tbsp (25 mL)
Fresh parsley	1 Tbsp (15 ml) finely chopped

1 Prepare the fish by cutting the fillets into strips approximately 1 inch (2.5 cm) wide.

2 Peel the potatoes and dice into small pieces. Heat 1 Tbsp (15 mL) of the oil in a frying pan or wok. Gently fry the diced potatoes for approximately 10 minutes, turning them to brown on all sides. Mix in 1 tsp (5 mL) of the salt.

3 Add the mushroom caps to the potatoes and cook for approximately 3 minutes. Add the diced cucumber and cook for another 3 minutes.

4 While the potatoes are frying, dredge the strips of fish in the flour to which 1 tsp (5 mL) of salt has been added.

5 In another frying pan melt 1 Tbsp (15 mL) of the butter and add the remaining 1/2 Tbsp (7.5 L) of oil. When the foam subsides, add the strips of floured fish. Fry gently until brown on all sides; this will take about 5 minutes. Drain off excess fat and transfer the fish to a warm serving dish. Mound the fish in the centre of the dish and spoon the vegetables around the fish.

6 Melt the remaining butter in the frying pan and just when it begins to turn golden, pour it over the vegetables. Sprinkle the fish with chopped parsley.

Serves 4

POTATO HEALTH LOAF

Mashed potatoes work well here because they are easy to shape into a loaf and combine well with a range of other ingredients. Half a cup of grated carrots may be added for colour and extra flavour.

Oil	2 tsp (10 mL)
Chopped walnuts	1 Tbsp (15 mL)
Mashed potatoes	2 cups (500 mL)
Onion	1, peeled and grated
Eggs	2, beaten
Soy flour	2 Tbsp (25 mL)
Fresh mixed herbs (e.g. parsley, chives, dill)	2 Tbsp (25 mL)
Milk powder	1/2 cup (125 mL)
Wheat germ	1/2 cup (125 mL)
Salt	1/2 tsp (2 mL)

Preheat oven to 350°F (180°C).

1 Pour 1 tsp (5 mL) of the oil on the walnuts and roll them gently to coat. Set aside.

2 Combine all the other ingredients, blending well by hand.

3 Sprinkle the chopped walnuts on the bottom of an oiled loaf pan. Spoon the potato mixture on top and press down firmly.

4 Bake at 350°F (180°C) for about 25 minutes.

5 Run a sharp knife around the inside of the baking tin to release the loaf. Tap the pan gently along the bottom and carefully turn the loaf out onto a serving dish, the walnut-coated side up.

Serves 4

POTATO AND HAM ROLLS

For a simple, yet satisfying summer lunch or brunch, serve these potato and ham rolls with a crisp, green salad. The potato filling is best made the night before, to allow the flavours to blend.

Potatoes	6 medium
Fresh chives or parsley	1 Tbsp (15 mL) finely chopped
English cucumber	1, peeled and diced
Salt	1/2 tsp (2 mL)
Eggs	2, hard-boiled
Butter	1 tsp (5 mL)
Onion	1, peeled and finely chopped
Mild curry powder	1 tsp (5 mL)
Mayonnaise	1 cup (250 mL)
Cooked ham	8 slices
Toothpicks	8

1 Boil the potatoes in their skins and peel them as soon as they are cool enough to handle. Dice them into pieces no larger than about 1/2-inch (1.25-cm) square.

2 In a large bowl combine the diced potatoes, chopped herbs, diced cucumber and salt. Chop the eggs finely and add to the bowl.

3 In a small frying pan melt the butter. When the foam subsides, add the chopped onions. Fry gently for 2 minutes, then add the curry powder. Fry for 5 minutes longer over low heat.

4 Remove the pan from the heat and allow to cool for a few minutes. Then add the curry and onion mixture to the mayonnaise and blend thoroughly.

5 Spoon the mayonnaise onto the potato mixture and gently fold in.

6 Spread the slices of ham on a flat surface and spoon one-eighth of the potato mixture in the centre of each slice of ham. Arrange the mixture in a funnel shape — with more mixture at one end than the other. Roll the ham into a cornet shape and secure with a toothpick.

Makes 8 rolls

POTATO STRUDEL

Here's an international mixture combining ingredients commonly found in the foods of Germany, India and the Middle East. It's easy to make, inexpensive and unquestionably delicious. Packages of phylo pastry are sold in most food stores, sometimes as phylo, sometimes as strudel dough.

If you prefer to make up your own curry powder, a suggested mixture of spices appears at the end of this recipe.

Leek	1
Butter	1 Tbsp (15 mL)
Onion	1, peeled and finely chopped
Zucchini (courgette)	2, washed, trimmed and grated
Curry powder	3 tsp (15 mL)
Potatoes	3 medium, boiled and coarsely chopped
Garlic	1 clove, minced
Eggs	2, beaten
Mashed potatoes	2 cups (500 mL)
Lemon juice	1 tsp (5 mL)
Salt	1 tsp (5 mL)
Cauliflower	1/4 small head
Phylo pastry	10 sheets
Butter for pastry	1/3 cup (75 mL) melted

Preheat oven to 350°F (180°C).

1 Trim off the rough, green sections of the leek, retaining only the white interior leaves and the tenderest green parts. Cut off the root. With a sharp knife, slice the leek in half lengthwise to expose the inner leaves. Hold under running water and separate the leaves to wash out all grit that clings to them. Chop the leek coarsely.

2 In a large frying pan melt the butter. Add the chopped leeks and onions and sweat gently for 20 minutes. While the leeks and onions are cooking, squeeze out any excess moisture from the grated zucchini.

3 Stir the curry powder into the onions and leeks and cook over gentle heat. Add the zucchini and continue cooking for a few minutes. Add the chopped boiled potatoes and minced garlic. Combine well and cook over moderate heat for about 5 minutes longer.

4 In a mixing bowl combine the beaten eggs, mashed potatoes, lemon juice and salt. Stir in the curried vegetables from the frying pan and combine thoroughly, being careful not to break up the boiled potatoes.

5 Chop the cauliflower into bite-size pieces and add to the other vegetables.

6 Set aside the mixture while you prepare the sheets of phylo.

7 Clear a work space approximately 2-feet (60-cm) square. Have the melted butter and a pastry brush close at hand. It's important to work quickly because the phylo sheets dry out and become brittle as soon as they are exposed to the air. Keep the extra sheets of pastry well covered or wrapped in a damp cloth.

8 Lay a clean teatowel on the work area. Place one sheet of phylo on the towel. Quickly brush the sheet with melted butter and add a second sheet on top. Once the pastry sheet has been brushed with butter it ceases to be brittle and the sheets stick together firmly. Continue to layer, brushing each sheet with butter and overlapping each additional sheet so that the final size of the layered pastry is a little larger than a single sheet. This extra size allows a generous overlap when you enclose the filling.

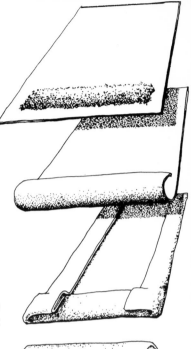

9 Place the pastry with a narrow edge closest to you. Starting 2 inches (5 cm) from the edge, spread the vegetable mixture over one-third of the pastry. Leave an uncovered border of at least 2 1/2 inches (6 cm) along each length of the pastry. Begin to roll by lifting the teatowel at the end closest to you. This action lifts the pastry over the filling. After the rolling has taken one turn, brush with melted butter and fold in the pastry flaps at each end, over the filling, parcel fashion. Continue to roll the filling into the pastry until the filling is completely wrapped and you have a neat, oblong parcel. Brush with melted butter. Carefully lift the roll onto a shallow baking dish (not a cookie sheet as some of the butter seeps out during cooking and will drip into the oven).

10 Bake at 350°F (180°C) for 40 minutes. Check after 25 minutes. If it is browning unevenly, turn the baking dish around.

11 Lift onto a serving dish and cut into thick slices.

Serves 4–6

CURRY MIXTURE

For the quantity required in this recipe combine 1/2 tsp (2 mL) of each of the following ground spices and mix well: cumin, turmeric, fenugreek and coriander seeds. To this mixture add 1/4 tsp (1 mL) each of ground nutmeg, ground cinnamon, ground ginger and cayenne and blend well.

SUNDAY PIE

When Rick and I wrote our earlier book, *The Pie's the Limit*, we missed including this delicious savoury pie. I'm delighted to have this chance to share a recipe which has been a favourite in my family for several generations.

Shortcrust Pastry

All-purpose flour	2 cups (500 mL) sifted
Salt	1/2 tsp (2 mL)
Butter/lard mixture	2/3 cup (150 mL)
Iced water	3 Tbsp (50 mL)

1 Sift together the flour and salt into a mixing bowl.

2 Cut in the butter and lard with a pastry blender or fork until the fat is broken into small pieces. Finish off the rubbing-in process with your fingertips. Rub the fat into the flour until the mixure resembles the texture of breadcrumbs. Make a well in the centre.

3 Into this well add some of the water and gradually draw the mixture into the liquid, using a fork or fingers. Add more water as necessary until the mixture comes away from the sides of the bowl and holds together. Press the dough into a ball, handling it as little as possible.

4 Rest the ball of dough in the refrigerator for 30 minutes. It will then be ready to roll.

Filling

Leeks	2
Onion	1 medium, coarsely chopped
Bacon	3 strips
Potatoes	4 medium
Cream	3/4 cup (175 mL)
Fresh parsley	1 Tbsp (15 mL) finely chopped
Salt	1/2 tsp (2 mL)
Pepper	1/4 tsp (1 mL)
Milk	1 Tbsp (15 mL)

Preheat oven to 400°F (200°C).

1 Divide the pastry into two portions, one a little larger than the other. Roll out each portion into a circle. Line a 9-inch (23-cm) pie dish with the larger circle of rolled dough. Set aside the lined pie dish and the smaller circle of pastry in the refrigerator to rest while you prepare the filling.

2 Trim off the rough, green sections of the leeks, retaining only the white interior leaves and the tenderest green parts. Cut off the root. With a sharp knife, slice the leeks in half lengthwise to expose the inner leaves. Hold under running water and separate the leaves to wash out all the grit that clings to them. Chop the leeks coarsely.

3 In a medium-sized frying pan fry the bacon strips for 5 minutes. Remove the bacon and cut into 1-inch (2.5-cm) pieces.

4 Pour off the bacon fat from the pan, reserving enough in the pan to fry the leeks and onions.

5 Sweat the chopped leeks and onions in the reserved bacon fat until soft. Mix in the bacon pieces and set aside.

6 Peel the potatoes and cut them into 1/4-inch (6-mm) slices.

7 Remove the pastry-lined pie dish from the refrigerator and spread a layer of sliced potatoes across the bottom. Spread a layer of the leek, bacon and onion mixture over the potatoes. Top with the remaining potato slices.

8 Beat the egg well. Add the cream, parsley, salt and pepper and stir together. Pour the mixture over the filling.

9 With a little milk moisten the pastry around the rim of the pie dish. Place the second circle of pastry over the filling and press the edges together or seal. Trim off any excess pastry around the edge and brush the top with milk. Pierce the top crust twice with a fork to allow steam to escape.

10 Bake at 400°F (200°C) for 30 minutes. Reduce the heat to 350°F (180°C) and bake for another 30 minutes.

Serves 6

CREAMY SMOKED COD AND POTATOES

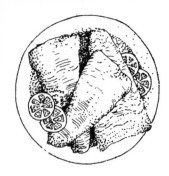

The pungent tang of smoked fish blends well with the cheese and eggs to make an interesting brunch or supper dish.

Smoked cod	1 lb (450 g)
Butter	1 Tbsp (15 mL)
Onion	1 medium, finely chopped
Milk	1 cup (250 mL) plus 2 Tbsp (25 mL)
Potatoes	3 large, diced
Flour	1 Tbsp (15 mL)
Eggs	3, hard-boiled
Medium Cheddar cheese	1/2 cup (125 mL) grated
Salt	1/2 tsp (2 mL)
Pepper	1/2 tsp (2 mL)
Fresh parsley	1 Tbsp (15 mL) finely chopped

1 Soak the cod in water and a little milk for 20 minutes. Pour off the liquid. Place the fish on a rack or steamer and steam over boiling water for about 10 minutes. Drain and keep warm while you make the sauce.

2 Melt the butter in a large, heavy saucepan. Add the chopped onions and fry gently until transparent. Add one cup of milk and the diced potatoes. Cover and cook over moderate heat for 10 minutes.

3 Pour 2 Tbsp (25 mL) of cold milk into a small cup or bowl. Mix with the flour to make a smooth, lump-free paste. Gradually blend the paste into the potato mixture in the saucepan, stirring as you add it. Continue to stir as the sauce thickens. Simmer gently for about 3 minutes to cook the flour.

4 Flake the fish into large pieces and fold into the potato mixture. Peel the eggs and chop them into quarters. Add them to the fish and potato mixture, along with the grated cheese, salt, pepper and chopped parsley. Mix gently, taking care not to break up the fish and eggs.

5 Warm through and serve.

Serves 4

PEAS AND POTATOES

This soothing, creamy concoction seems to remind many of my friends of their childhood, although I don't ever remember having this particular combination when I was a child.

Butter	3 Tbsp (50 mL)
Onion	1 medium, peeled and finely sliced
Evaporated milk	1 cup (250 mL)
Potatoes	3 large, peeled and cubed
Peas	1 cup (250 mL), cooked or frozen
Salt	1 tsp (5 mL)
Pepper	1/4 tsp (1 mL)
Fresh parsley	1 Tbsp (15 mL) finely chopped

1 Melt the butter in a large saucepan. When the foam subsides, add the sliced onions and fry them over moderate heat for about 5 minutes or until transparent.

2 Add the evaporated milk and potatoes to the pot. Cover tightly and simmer for 15 to 20 minutes or until the potatoes are tender. Add a little milk if the liquid evaporates.

3 Add the cooked or frozen peas, salt and pepper and continue to cook for about 5 to 7 minutes or until the peas are tender. Stir in the chopped parsley.

Serves 4

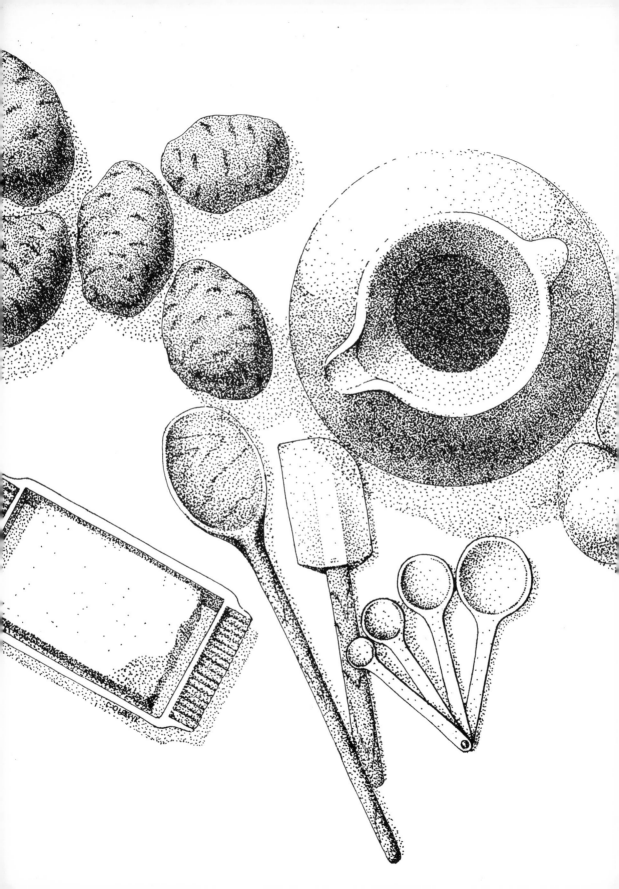

SIDE DISHES

Not Just Potato and Two Veg

For many people, no matter how elaborately the food is prepared, a meal must include meat and potatoes. Other vegetables may come and go, the victims of whim and fashion, but potatoes are basic to the concept of a western meal.

Drop potatoes from the menu at your peril. Your guests will mutter about it for weeks and may decline your next invitation to dine. In this book we aim to show that potatoes are more than just an accompaniment, but for many, the main role of the potato is as a side dish. After all, if you find yourself short of meat or fish, you can always "fill 'em up" with quantities of potato.

As a side dish, potatoes leave plenty of room for self-expression. The recipes we give lend themselves to many variations. The addition of a beaten egg or grated cheese or fresh chopped herbs can make a wonderful difference to mashed potatoes. You might sprinkle boiled potatoes with tender mint leaves or paprika or sunflower seeds.

In this chapter you'll find a variety of dishes, some more elaborate than others, but all easy to prepare. There are many classic potato dishes using mashed potatoes — Duchess, Chantilly, Dauphine — you'll find them all here. As a useful rule of thumb, three medium potatoes make about 2 cups (500 mL) of mashed potatoes. Basic information about boiling, baking and roasting potatoes can be found in the introduction at the beginning of the book.

Side Dishes

GREEK POTATOES

Vegetables hold a place of honour in Greek cuisine and for almost any vegetable you can think of, there is at least one recipe with the fragrant accompaniment of garlic, lemon juice and oil. Potatoes are no exception. You can use your favourite cooking oil, but a light olive oil will add a touch of authenticity.

Garlic	3 cloves, minced
Oil	1/3 cup (75 mL)
Potatoes	6 medium
Lemon juice	1/2 cup (125 mL)
Fresh oregano	1 Tbsp (15 mL) finely chopped
Salt	1 tsp (5 mL)
Pepper	1/2 tsp (2 mL) freshly ground

Preheat oven to 350°F (180°C).

1 Rub the surface of a shallow baking dish with the minced garlic, leaving the garlic in the dish when you've finished rubbing it in. Pour in the oil.

2 Peel and slice the potatoes into rounds about 1/4 inch (6 mm) thick. Dip each slice in the oil, coating it on both sides. Arrange the slices in the dish so that they just overlap.

3 Pour on the lemon juice, sprinkle with oregano, salt and pepper and cover with aluminum foil.

4 Bake at 350°F (180°C) for about 1 hour. Remove the foil for the last 20 minutes of cooking.

Serves 4

POTATO GNOCCHI

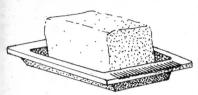

When making gnocchi, it's important to keep the mixture as dry as possible. After the potatoes have been boiled, drain off the water and let the pot sit on the stove for a minute on low heat to allow the excess moisture to evaporate. Watch the potatoes don't burn. Unless the mixture is dry, the gnocchi will disintegrate as they poach.

Potatoes	6 large, boiled and peeled
Garlic	2 cloves, minced
Fresh parsley	2 Tbsp (25 mL) finely chopped
Butter	1 Tbsp (15 mL)
Salt	1/2 tsp (2 mL)
Pepper	1/4 tsp (1 mL)
All-purpose flour	1 cup (250 mL)
Eggs	2, beaten
Parmesan cheese	1/3 cup (75 mL) grated

Preheat oven to 350°F (180°C).

1 Using a food mill or an electric beater make a purée of the potatoes, garlic, parsley, butter, salt and pepper. Make a well in the centre and gradually add flour.

2 When the flour has been mixed in thoroughly, add the beaten eggs and mix well. Set the mixture aside for a few minutes.

3 Fill a very large saucepan with water, add a little salt and bring to a boil.

4 Shape the potato mixture into small dumplings and drop them into the boiling water, a few at a time. They will rise to the surface when they're cooked.

5 Drain the gnocchi well and spoon into an oven-proof serving dish. Sprinkle with grated Parmesan and dot with a little butter.

6 Bake in the centre of a moderate oven 350°F (180°C) for about 5 minutes.

Serves 6

Top: Aloo Gobi with Fried Onions (see page 72)
Bottom: Aloo Raita (see page 52)

DANISH POTATOES

My cousin Dianne introduced us to these potatoes in Australia. Last summer during a visit to Denmark, we sought them out and in so doing learned their secret: Danish potatoes (katofflers) are very, very waxy. In the absence of Danish potatoes use very new, or waxy local potatoes so that the caramelized sugar will coat the potatoes evenly.

New potatoes	2 lbs (900 g), uniform sizes
Sugar	1 cup (250 mL)
Butter	1/2 cup (125 mL)
Fresh dill	1/4 cup (50 mL) finely chopped

1 Scrub the potatoes and cook in boiling water for approximately 10 minutes. Drain the potatoes and run them under cold water. Peel and set aside.

2 In a large, heavy saucepan, heat the sugar over low heat until it melts. When it turns a light caramel colour, add the butter and allow it to melt.

3 Add the potatoes and toss them until they are evenly coated with the caramel mixture.

4 Serve sprinkled with dill.

Serves 4

HUNGARIAN PAN-FRY

On a recent trip to central Europe and the Soviet Union I noted that potatoes appeared in copious quantities at every meal. It was not surprising to see potatoes, after all they are a staple in Europe, but it was very interesting to see the many inventive ways in which they were prepared. This is one of them.

Potatoes	4 medium
Onion	2 medium
Bacon	2 strips
Sweet paprika	1 tsp (5 mL)
Salt	1 tsp (5 mL)
Pepper	1/4 tsp (1 mL)
Sour cream	1 1/4 cups (300 mL)

1 Peel the potatoes and cut into 1/2-inch (1.25-cm) cubes. Peel and finely chop the onions.

2 In a large frying pan fry the bacon for about 5 minutes. Remove the bacon and set aside. Add the chopped onions and fry in the bacon fat for about 7 minutes or until transparent. While the onions are frying, add the paprika, salt and pepper and stir through.

3 Remove the frying pan from the heat and stir the sour cream thoroughly into the onion mixture. Chop the bacon into small pieces and add to the pan.

4 Mix in the cubed potatoes and combine well with the onions and sour cream. Cover the pan and cook over gentle heat for about 30 minutes. Do not allow the sour cream to boil. Occasionally stir the potatoes to coat them with the sauce and to cook them evenly.

Serves 4

RED AND GREEN PAN-FRY

This recipe can be extended easily by adding whatever vegetables you may have on hand. The combination of red and green makes a particularly attractive dish.

Red-skinned potatoes	8–10 small
Red onion	1 medium
Broccoli	1 head
Butter	2 Tbsp (25 mL)
Zucchini (courgettes)	2 medium, sliced
Salt	1 tsp (5 mL)
Pepper	1/2 tsp (2 mL)

1 Scrub the potatoes and boil them in their skins for about 15 minutes or until cooked but still firm. Drain and set aside.

2 Peel the onion and slice it into rings.

3 Trim off the coarse parts of the broccoli stem and discard. Slice the tender parts of the stem and cut up the head into individual florets.

4 Melt the butter in a large pan or wok. Add the onion rings and stir fry for about 5 minutes. Add the sliced broccoli and zucchini and toss them in the butter. Add the potatoes and season with salt and pepper. Toss gently and stir fry for about 5 minutes; the greens should be slightly crunchy.

Serves 4

HASSELBACK POTATOES

Not only are hasselback potatoes easy to prepare, they have an interesting appearance. They may be topped with extras such as grated cheese, breadcrumbs, crisp bacon bits or chopped herbs.

Potatoes	6 large, peeled
Butter	2 Tbsp (25 mL) melted
Oil	1 Tbsp (15 mL)
Salt	1/2 tsp (2 mL)
Cheddar or Swiss cheese	1 cup (250 mL) grated
Dry breadcrumbs	1/2 cup (125 mL)

Preheat oven to 350°F (180°C).

1 Place the peeled potatoes horizontally on a chopping board and slice them vertically, cutting only three-quarters of the way through. Make the slices about 1/4 inch (6 mm) apart. This keeps the potato in one piece, but allows it to fan out as it cooks.

2 Pour the melted butter and oil into a shallow baking pan — one large enough to hold all the potatoes in a single layer without crowding.

3 Dredge each potato with the butter and oil to coat evenly. Arrange the potatoes, cut sides up, in the pan. Sprinkle with salt.

4 Bake at 350°F (180°C) for about 45 minutes. Baste them frequently with the oil and butter from the pan.

5 Continue to bake for 15 minutes without basting, to produce a slight crust on the surface.

6 Mix together the grated cheese and breadcrumbs and spoon over the potatoes, allowing the mixture to settle into each cut. Bake until the cheese has melted and the breadcrumbs have browned — about 10 minutes.

Serves 6

RISSOLÉE POTATOES

Margarine is better than butter for this recipe since margarine has a higher smoke point than butter. Butter will smoke at an oven temperature of 400°F (200°C).

Potatoes	6 large
Margarine	4 Tbsp (50 mL)

Preheat oven to 400°F (200°C).

1 Peel the potatoes and rinse them well under cold water. Cut each potato crosswise in half and, with a vegetable knife, cut the halves into even sizes. The traditional method is to trim the halves into barrel shapes, but this is not necessary.

2 Blanch the potatoes in boiling water for 5 minutes. Drain well.

3 In a large frying pan melt the margarine and fry the potatoes for about 5 minutes over moderate heat. Toss well to coat them thoroughly with the margarine.

4 Transfer the potatoes to a shallow baking pan and complete the cooking in a 400°F (200°C) oven for 30 minutes or until the potatoes have cooked through. Turn them several times while cooking to brown them evenly.

Serves 6

PIQUANT NEW POTATOES

New potatoes are wonderful just boiled with a little salt and fresh mint. But if you want to take them one step further, here is a suggestion. By the way, never peel new potatoes.

New potatoes	1 lb (450 g), uniform size
Butter	2 Tbsp (25 mL)
Green onion	1, finely chopped
Dijon mustard	1 tsp (5 mL)
Fresh parsley	1 Tbsp (15 mL) finely chopped
Fresh chives	1 Tbsp (15 mL) finely chopped
Salt	1/2 tsp (2 mL)
Pepper	1/2 tsp (2 mL)

1 Scrub the potatoes and cook in boiling salted water for 15 to 20 minutes, depending on the size. Test with a fork; if it penetrates easily, the potatoes are done. Drain well.

2 In a frying pan melt the butter and add the chopped green onions. Cook for about one minute, then add the mustard, chopped parsley and chives, salt and pepper. Blend well.

3 Add the potatoes. Toss them in the flavoured butter and coat well.

Serves 4

KIRSTEN'S POTATO CAKES

When we make mashed potatoes in our family, we make plenty of them because there will always be someone hovering over the leftovers. Rick's daughter Kirsten, inventive as ever, devised this recipe to satisfy all leftover lovers . . . so to speak.

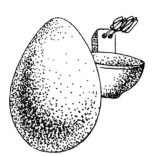

Mashed potatoes	3 cups (750 mL)
Butter	2 Tbsp (25 mL)
Egg	1, beaten
Nutmeg	1/4 tsp (1 mL) freshly grated
Salt	1 tsp (5 mL)
Flour	1 Tbsp (15 mL)
Oil	1 Tbsp (15 mL)
Parmesan cheese	3 Tbsp (50 mL) grated

1 Combine the mashed potatoes, one Tbsp (15 mL) of the butter, the beaten egg, nutmeg and salt and mix well.

2 Lightly coat your hands with flour and shape the mixture into round cakes about 1 inch (2.5 cm) thick.

3 Heat the remaining butter and the oil in a large frying pan. Fry the cakes over moderate heat until browned on both sides.

4 Drain on paper towels to absorb excess fat. Serve sprinkled with Parmesan cheese.

Makes about 8 cakes

POTATO AND SALMON FRITTERS

Eggs	3
Onion	1 medium, minced or grated
Mashed potatoes	2 cups (500 mL)
Salmon	1 can, 6.5-oz (184-g), drained
Flour	3 Tbsp (50 mL)
Salt	1/2 tsp (2 mL)
Lemon juice	1 tsp (5 mL)
Dry breadcrumbs	1 cup (250 mL)
Oil	for deep frying

1 In a large mixing bowl beat two of the eggs.

2 Squeeze the minced onions in a paper towel to remove the moisture and add to the beaten egg.

3 Combine the mashed potatoes with the egg mixture and stir in the drained salmon. Add the flour, salt and lemon juice and blend thoroughly. Divide the mixture into 10 small balls. Shape the balls by hand into flat, round cakes. Refrigerate for about 30 minutes.

4 In a small bowl mix the remaining egg with a little water and beat well to make an egg wash. Spread the breadcrumbs on a dinner plate.

5 Dip each cake into the egg wash and coat well, then roll it in the breadcrumbs. Set the cake aside on a plate until all have been coated. Repeat the coating process to give a firm seal.

6 Deep fry the fritters in hot oil. The fritters will rise to the surface when they are cooked.

Makes 10 fritters

POTATOES ANNA

This classic dish, a crisp potato cake, may be sliced and served as a side dish or topped with breadcrumbs and grated cheese and served with a green salad for a satisfying lunch.

Potatoes Anna can be made more quickly in a frying pan on top of the stove, although turning the potato cake in the pan to crisp both sides requires some dexterity. Alternatively, you can crisp the top by putting it under the broiler.

Potatoes	5 large, peeled
Salt	1 tsp (5 mL)
Clarified butter	3/4 cup (175 mL)
Pepper	1/4 tsp (1 mL)

Preheat oven to 425°F (220°C).

1 Cut the potatoes paper thin by hand or with a food processor.

2 Cover the potatoes with cold water and soak for 10 minutes. Rinse several times. Drain and dry well with paper towels. Sprinkle with salt.

3 Melt the clarified butter in an oven-proof casserole dish or cake tin. Roll the butter around in the dish to coat the inside surface. Once the dish has been coated, pour off the excess butter into a small bowl and set aside.

4 Arrange an overlapping layer of the sliced potatoes across the bottom of the dish. Press the layer down with the back of a spoon.

5 Using a pastry brush dipped in the melted butter, brush the potatoes generously. Arrange another overlapping layer on top and press it down. Brush with the butter and repeat the layers, brushing each with butter until all the potatoes have been used. Press the potatoes down firmly.

6 Bake, covered, in a hot oven for approximately 35 minutes. Remove the cover, press down firmly again and continue baking until the top is crisp — approximately another 20 to 30 minutes.

7 With a knife loosen the potatoes from the edges of the dish. Drain off any excess butter and invert onto a serving dish.

Serves 4

SCALLOPED POTATOES

The combination of potatoes, milk and herbs makes a distinctive but delicate addition to any main course. The soothing creaminess won't fight with other flavours, and the dish doesn't call for any last-minute fiddling. It goes straight from oven to table, with a garnish of chopped parsley or mixed herbs to add a little colour.

There are many variations of scalloped potatoes, with all manner of additions, but this is the basic recipe. Add what you like to make it a main course, but be careful of vegetables which contain a lot of water (such as mushrooms or tomatoes). If you use them, you may have to cut down a little on the milk or you'll find you have made soup!

Butter	1 Tbsp (15 mL)
Garlic	1 clove, peeled
Potatoes	4 medium
Milk	1 1/2 cups (375 mL)
Salt	1/4 tsp (1 mL)
Fresh parsley or mixed herbs	1 Tbsp (15 mL) finely chopped

Preheat oven to 350°F (180°C).

1 Rub a shallow, oven-proof dish with a little butter and the clove of garlic. Press the garlic into the dish as you rub to release the aroma.

2 Peel the potatoes and cut into even slices not more than 1/4 inch (6 mm) thick.

3 Arrange the potato slices in layers in the dish, sprinkling each layer with a little salt. Dot the top with butter and pour on the milk.

4 Bake at 350°F (180°C) for about 1 hour. Sprinkle with chopped parsley or your choice of mixed herbs and serve.

Serves 4

PIGS IN BLANKETS

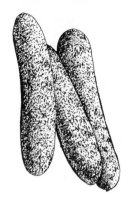

There are many versions of pigs in blankets, each an ingenious combination of pork sausages rolled in something such as pancakes or pastry. In this case the covering is potato.

Potatoes	4 large, scrubbed
Pork sausages	4, long and thin
Bacon	4 strips

Preheat oven to 400°F (200°C).

1 Parboil the sausages for 5 minutes. Drain and set aside.

2 Using an apple corer, bore out a hole through the length of each potato and ease a sausage through the hole.

3 Place the potatoes on a lightly oiled baking sheet and bake at 400°F (200°C) for 45 minutes. Remove from the oven and wrap a strip of bacon around each potato (securing with a tooth pick if necessary). Continue baking at 375°F (190°C) for 10 minutes or until the bacon has cooked.

Serves 4

CRADLED SAUSAGES

Baking potatoes	4 large, scrubbed
Salt	1 tsp (5 mL)
Prepared mustard	1 tsp (5 mL)
Milk	2 Tbsp (25 mL)
Butter	1 Tbsp (15 mL)
Pork sausages	12 cocktail-size, parboiled for 5 minutes

Preheat oven to 375°F (190°C).

1 Bake the potatoes at 375°F (190°C) according to the instructions on page 109. When the potatoes have cooked, cut a thick slice off the length of each potato. Scoop out the pulp, leaving a little pulp attached to the skin for support.

2 In a mixing bowl combine the pulp from the potatoes, salt, mustard, milk and butter. Beat together thoroughly.

3 Return the pulp to the potato shells, leaving room to place 3 small sausages, side by side across the opening of each.

4 Transfer the potatoes to a baking sheet and return them to the oven. Bake at 375°F (190°C) for about 20 minutes or until the sausages are cooked.

Serves 4

BAKED POTATOES

If you like your baked potatoes with crisp skins, don't wrap them in foil. They bake best if they are simply scrubbed and pricked a few times with a fork to allow the steam to escape. Bake them on a low rack in the oven for a crisper skin — the longer it bakes, the crisper the skin becomes. An average-sized baking potato takes about 1 hour to cook at 375°F (190°C). The potatoes should be turned over half-way through the cooking time. To test if they are done, press them between your thumb and fingers; they should feel soft right through.

Simple Baked Potatoes

When the potatoes are cooked, with a sharp knife cut off a thin slice along the top and add seasonings to taste. Alternatively, cut a large X in the top and press the sides together to enlarge the opening. Some traditional toppings are butter, salt and pepper, or sour cream and herbs.

Stuffed Baked Potatoes

To make a slightly fancy version of the baked potato, slice the potatoes in half lengthwise and scoop out the soft pulp in the centre and transfer the pulp to a mixing bowl. Leave a little pulp attached to the skin to give support.

Mash the potato pulp or put it through a food mill or ricer. Don't use a blender or food processor; the result will be like glue. Add salt, pepper, butter and seasonings to the mashed potatoes. The seasonings might include any number of the following: grated cheese, chopped herbs, fried mushrooms, fried onions, cooked bacon bits, chopped cooked ham, cottage cheese. Spoon the seasoned pulp back into the potato skins and place them on a baking sheet. Reheat in a moderate oven (350°F, 180°C) for about 10 minutes.

BAKED POTATOES WITH BACON

Baking potatoes	4
Butter	2 Tbsp (25 mL)
Sour cream or milk	4 Tbsp (60 mL)
Salt	1/2 tsp (2 mL)
Pepper or cayenne	1/4 tsp (1 mL)
Bacon	6 slices, fried crisp and chopped
Cheddar cheese	1/2 cup (125 mL) grated

Preheat oven to 375°F (190°C).

1 Bake the potatoes at 375°F (190°C) according to the instructions on page 000.

2 Cut the potatoes horizontally into halves. Scoop out the soft centres into a mixing bowl, leaving some pulp attached to the skin for support. Set the potato skins aside while you prepare the filling.

3 Mash the potato pulp with the butter, sour cream, salt and pepper. Stir in the chopped bacon.

4 Transfer the mashed potato mixture back into the skins and top with grated cheese.

5 Preheat the oven to 350°F (180°C). Place the stuffed potatoes on a baking sheet and bake in the oven for 15 minutes or until the cheese is bubbling.

Makes 8 halves

BEEFY BAKED POTATOES

Baking potatoes	4 large
Bacon	4 strips, cut in half
Onions	2 medium, peeled and finely chopped
Lean ground beef	1/2lb (225 g)
Tomato paste	2 Tbsp (25 mL)
Salt	1 tsp (5 mL)
Pepper	1/2 tsp (2 mL)
Red wine or sherry	1 Tbsp (15 mL)
Celery	2 stalks, finely chopped

Preheat oven to 375°F (190°C).

1 Bake the potatoes at 375°F (190°C) according to the instructions on page 109.

2 While the potatoes are baking, fry the bacon until crisp, in a large frying pan. Set aside the bacon and pour off the excess fat from the pan. Add the onions to the pan and fry over moderate heat until transparent.

3 Add the ground beef and stir fry until it begins to brown. Add the tomato paste, salt, pepper and wine and stir through the meat. Cook over moderate heat for 15 minutes.

4 Add the celery, mix well and cook for another 10 minutes. Set aside until the potatoes have cooked.

5 When the potatoes have cooked, cut them lengthwise into halves. Scoop out the pulp into a large mixing bowl, but leave a little pulp attached to the potato skin for support.

6 Combine the savoury meat with the potato pulp and mix together thoroughly.

7 Preheat the oven to 350°F (180°C). Spoon the mixture back into the potato shells. Arrange the potato halves on a baking sheet and bake in the oven for about 15 minutes to heat through. During the last 2 minutes of cooking, top each potato with a strip of crisp bacon.

Serves 8

SUMMER BAKE

Potatoes	4 large
Red onion	1 small, peeled and finely chopped
Green pepper	1 small, cored and finely chopped
Cheddar cheese	1 cup (250 mL) grated
Salt	1 tsp (5 mL)
Pepper	1/2 tsp (2 mL)
Fresh parsley	1 Tbsp (15 mL) finely chopped
Butter	1 Tbsp (15 mL)
Fresh garlic chives	1 Tbsp (15 mL) finely chopped
Lemon juice	2 tsp (10 mL)
Egg	1, beaten

Preheat oven to 375°F (190°C).

1 Bake the potatoes at 375°F (190°C) according to the instructions on page 109 . While the potatoes are baking, prepare the ingredients for the filling.

2 In a large bowl combine the chopped onions, green pepper, cheese, salt, pepper, parsley, butter and chives and mix thoroughly.

3 When the potatoes have cooked, with a sharp knife cut off a thick lid from each top. Lift off the lid carefully and set it aside. Scoop out the soft pulp from the centre of each potato and add it to the contents of the bowl. Leave a little pulp attached to the skin for support. Mash the pulp into the chopped ingredients and add the lemon juice. Beat in the beaten egg.

4 Preheat the oven to 350°F (180°C). Spoon the mixture into the potato shells and replace the lids. Arrange the potatoes on a baking sheet and heat in the oven for 12–15 minutes until the potatoes are warmed through. Serve immediately.

Serves 4

BAKED POTATOES
WITH A HEART

Potatoes	4 large, scrubbed
Cream	1/3 cup (75 mL)
Butter	1 Tbsp (15 mL)
Fresh chives	1 Tbsp (15 mL) finely chopped
Salt	1 tsp (5 mL)
Pepper	1/4 tsp (1 mL)
Marinated artichoke hearts	8
Paprika	1 tsp (5 mL)

Preheat oven to 375°F (190°C).

1 Bake the potatoes at 375°F (190°C) according to the instructions on page 109 . When the potatoes have cooked, cut them horizontally into halves.

2 Scoop out the pulp from the centre of each potato, but leave a little pulp attached to the skin for support.

3 In a mixing bowl combine the pulp from the potatoes with the cream, butter, chives, salt and pepper and blend well. Spoon the mixture into the potato shells.

4 Drain the artichoke hearts and slice each one down the centre but not right through the bottom. Place one heart on each potato half and spread apart the heart to cover the centre of the filling.

5 Preheat the oven to 350°F (180°C). Arrange the halves on a baking sheet and bake in the oven for approximately 10 minutes. Sprinkle with paprika and serve hot.

Serves 8

SALMON-BAKED POTATOES

Potatoes	4 large, scrubbed
Butter	1 Tbsp (15 mL)
Milk	1/3 cup (75 mL)
Onion	1, peeled and grated
Lemon juice	1 Tbsp (15 mL)
Salt	1 tsp (5 mL)
Pepper	1/2 tsp (2 mL)
Salmon	1 can, 6.5-oz (184-g)
Cheddar cheese	1/2 cup (125 mL) grated

Preheat oven to 375°F (190°C).

1 Bake the potatoes at 375°F (190°C) according to the instructions on page 109.

2 When the potatoes have cooked, with a sharp knife cut off a thick lid from each top. Lift off the lid. Remove the pulp from the lid and discard the skin. Scoop out the soft pulp from the centre of each potato and place it in a mixing bowl. Leave a little pulp attached to the skin for support.

3 To the pulp in the mixing bowl add the butter, milk, onion, lemon juice, salt and pepper and combine well. Drain the salmon and break up the chunks into flakes. Add the salmon to the mixture and stir through.

4 Spoon the mixture into the potato shells and sprinkle each top with grated cheese.

5 Preheat the oven to 350°F (180°C). Arrange the potatoes on a baking sheet and heat in the oven for approximately 15 minutes.

Serves 4

BAKED POTATOES WITH A KICK

Potatoes	4 large, scrubbed
Butter	2 Tbsp (30 mL)
Barbecue sauce	1 Tbsp (15 mL)
Worcestershire sauce	1 tsp (5 mL)
Onion	1, peeled and grated
Fresh chives	1 Tbsp (15 mL) finely chopped
Salt	1 tsp (5 mL)
Pepper	1/2 tsp (2 mL)
Dry breadcrumbs	1/2 cup (125 mL)

Preheat oven to 375°F (190°C).

1 Bake the potatoes at 375°F (190°C) according to the instructions on page 109. When the potatoes have cooked, cut them horizontally into halves.

2 Scoop out the pulp from the centre of each potato, leaving a little pulp attached to the skin for support.

3 In a mixing bowl mash together the potato pulp, 1 Tbsp (15 mL) of the butter, the barbecue sauce and Worcestershire sauce, onion, chives, salt and pepper. Spoon the mixture into the shells.

4 Preheat the oven to 350°F (180°C). Arrange the potatoes on a baking sheet and top each with breadcrumbs and dot with the remaining butter. Bake in the oven for approximately 15 minutes.

Makes 8 halves

CRACKED POTATOES

When new potatoes are in season, try this unusual technique for pan frying.

Garlic	2 cloves
Oil	1/3 cup (75 mL)
New potatoes	2 lb (900 g)
Salt	1 tsp (5 mL)
Pepper	1/2 tsp (2 mL) freshly ground

1 Crush and peel the garlic and let it stand in the oil for approximately 1/2 an hour.

2 Wash the potatoes and dry them thoroughly. Crack each potato by hitting it with a kitchen mallet. Flatten out the potatoes as much as possible without disintegrating them.

3 In a large, heavy frying pan heat the oil and fry the potatoes for about 10 minutes on each side.

4 Drain on paper towels to absorb excess oil. Season with salt and freshly ground black pepper.

Serves 4

BUTTERED POTATOES

For this recipe you'll need a heavy saucepan with a tight-fitting lid. The aim is to steam the potatoes so that they pick up the flavour from the moisture in the onion. You will notice that there is only a small quantity of water added.

If you don't have a heavy saucepan, you will need to increase the quantity of water; but the more water you add, the more diluted the flavour will be.

Potatoes	4 medium
Onion	1 medium
Butter	2 Tbsp (25 mL)
Salt	1/2 tsp (2 mL)
Fresh dill	1 Tbsp (15 mL) finely chopped
Garlic	1 clove, minced
Cayenne, optional	a pinch
Water	3 Tbsp (50 mL)

1 Peel the potatoes and cut them into small, even-sized pieces. Peel the onion and chop finely.

2 Melt the butter in a saucepan with a tight-fitting lid. The saucepan should be large enough to contain all of the ingredients.

3 Sauté the chopped onions in the butter for a couple of minutes, then add the potatoes. Coat the potatoes with butter, then add the salt, dill, minced garlic, cayenne and water. Reserve a little of the dill for garnish.

4 Cover with the lid and cook over medium to low heat. Toss the potatoes occasionally to prevent them from sticking. Do not remove the lid unless it is necessary to add a little water.

5 Cook for approximately 30 minutes. Serve sprinkled with chopped dill.

Serves 4

DEEP-FRIED POTATOES (FRIES)

We all know about French fries, but there are many ways to chop a potato, so to speak. The following recipes are similar, but what is different is the thickness of the potato and the length of time required to cook each thickness. In domestic fryers, fries should be cooked a handful at a time so as not to crowd them and slow down the cooking time. Do not put a lid on any food that is deep frying, because steam will built on the inside surface of the lid producing water that dilutes the oil and causes spattering.

Deep Frying

There are two ways to deep fry potatoes. The first is simply to heat the oil to about 375°F (190°C) and cook the potatoes until they are done. The second method, the one preferred by most restaurants, involves two steps. First heat the oil to about 350°F (180°C) and cook the potatoes for 2 to 3 minutes. Lift the partially cooked potatoes out of the oil and drain them on paper towels. Increase the heat of the oil to 375°F (190°C) and refry the potatoes for about 3 minutes or until golden brown. This second method is best if you are making a large quantity, as it allows the first stage of the frying to be done in advance.

The oil should be deep enough to allow the potatoes to float freely.

Oven-Baked Fries

Potatoes may be baked in the oven instead of deep fried — a good idea if you are counting calories. Simply brush the potatoes with oil or an oil and butter mixture and spread them on greased baking sheets. Heat the oven to about 400°F (200°C) and bake the potatoes for 45 minutes to 1 hour, depending on the size and thickness. Turn the potatoes several times during the baking.

French Fries

Potatoes	4 large, scrubbed
Oil	for deep frying
Salt	1 tsp

1 Cut the potatoes (peeled or unpeeled, as you prefer) into sticks about 2'' × 1/2'' × 1/2'' (5 cm × 1.25 cm × 1.25 cm). Soak the potatoes in cold water for 5 minutes. Drain thoroughly and dry well on paper towels.

2 Deep fry by either method or bake in the oven. Directions are on page 118. Drain well and sprinkle with salt.

Bataille Potatoes

Ingredients same as above.

1 Peel the potatoes and cut them into 1/2-inch (1.25-cm) cubes. Soak the potatoes in cold water for 5 minutes. Drain thoroughly and dry on paper towels or in a salad spinner.

2 Deep fry by either method or bake in the oven. Directions are on page 118. Drain well and sprinkle with salt.

Straw Potatoes

Ingredients same as above.

1 Cut the potatoes very thinly into straws with either a food processor or mandoline. Soak the potatoes in cold water for 5 minutes. Drain thoroughly and dry on paper towels or in a salad spinner.

2 Since these straws are very thin, either bake them or use the one-step deep-frying method described on page 118. Drain well and sprinkle with salt.

Filettini

Ingredients same as above.

1 Cut the potatoes (peeled or unpeeled as you prefer) lengthwise into long, thin sticks. Soak the sticks in cold water for 5 minutes. Drain thoroughly and dry well on paper towels or in a salad spinner.

2 Since these fries are very thin either bake or use the one-step method for deep frying described on page 118. Drain well and sprinkle with salt.

Pont-Neuf Potatoes

Ingredients same as above.

1 Cut the peeled potatoes into thick strips about 2'' × 1'' × 1'' (5 cm × 2.5 cm × 2.5 cm). Soak the potatoes in cold water for 5 minutes. Drain thoroughly and dry well on paper towels. Pont-neuf potatoes are thick and will take longer to cook than the other types of fries.

2 Deep fry using the two-step method as described on page 118. Drain well and sprinkle with salt.

ARTHUR'S POTATOES IN PARSLEY BUTTER

Arthur Warner owns a bookstore in Newcastle, a city on the east coast of New South Wales where I grew up. In the early seventies Arthur made it into the Guinness Book of Records for eating the greatest quantity of potatoes in the shortest time. Any mention of that feat makes him blush these days, but when I exhorted him to give me his favourite potato recipe, he said, ''The simpler, the better.'' Here it is.

New potatoes	2 lb (900 g)
Butter	1/4 cup (50 mL)
Fresh parsley	3 Tbsp (50 mL) finely chopped
Salt	1/2 tsp (2 mL)
Pepper	1/2 tsp (2 mL)

1 In a large pot bring water to a boil and add salt. Cook the potatoes in the boiling water for 15 to 20 minutes, depending on the size. Test with a fork; if it penetrates easily, the potatoes are done. Drain well.

2 Melt the butter in a small saucepan. When the foam subsides, stir in the parsley, salt and pepper.

3 Transfer the potatoes to a serving dish and pour the parsley butter over them.

Serves 6

CHANTILLY POTATOES

A buffet centrepiece of steaming Chantilly potatoes is sure to evoke admiration. In classic French cooking the term "Chantilly" indicates the use of cream in a dish.

Potatoes	6, boiled and peeled
Butter	1 Tbsp (15 mL)
Whipping cream	1/2 cup (125 mL)
Sharp cheddar cheese	1/2 cup (125 mL) grated
Salt	1 tsp (5 mL)
Dry sherry	1 Tbsp (15 mL)
Nutmeg	1/4 tsp (1 mL) freshly grated
Dry breadcrumbs	1/2 cup (125 mL)

Preheat oven to 350°F (180°C).

1 Mash the potatoes with half the butter and half the cream. Beat in the cheese, salt, sherry and nutmeg.

2 Spoon the potato mixture into the centre of a shallow oven-proof serving dish and shape into a circular mound.

3 Carefully pour the remaining cream over the potatoes.

4 Sprinkle the breadcrumbs evenly over the potatoes and press in lightly so that they don't slide off. Dot with butter.

5 Bake in a moderate oven for approximately 20 minutes or until warmed through and lightly browned.

Serves 4–6

BASIC MASHED POTATOES

Any fool can mash a potato, you say; after all, it's like boiling water. But, I'm sure you'll agree that some people can mash them better than others. Here's how we do them in our house.

Potatoes cooked in their skins have more flavour, but it does take a little extra time to peel hot potatoes. If you are in a hurry, peel the potatoes before you boil them.

Potatoes	6 medium
Butter	3 Tbsp (50 mL)
Milk	1/3 cup (75 mL)
Salt	1 tsp (5 mL)
Pepper	1/2 tsp (2 mL)

1 Scrub the potatoes but do not peel them. Cut them into large pieces of approximately equal size. Place in a pot and add enough salted cold water to cover. Bring to a boil, then reduce heat to a simmer. Unless the pieces are very large, the potatoes should be cooked in 20 minutes. Test with a fork; if it penetrates easily, the potatoes are done.

2 Drain the potatoes immediately. They become waterlogged if they sit for any time once they are done. Return the drained potatoes to the pot. Cover with a cloth or paper towels and warm them over low heat for a few minutes to dry them out. Shake the pot if they seem to be sticking.

3 Once the potatoes have been cooked, you will find that the skins will lift off easily. Peel them and mash them by hand, adding the butter, milk, salt and pepper as you go. Mashed potatoes should be free of lumps, and a potato masher will do the job quickly and easily. If you like your mashed potatoes very creamy and smooth, whip them with a hand or electric beater, but do not use a blender or food processor or your potatoes may turn to glue.

Serves 4

Note: There are many variations to the mashed potato theme. I've listed a few of our favourites on the next page. In each case you should mash the potatoes first to remove any lumps. Then, blend in the other ingredients by hand.

Variations on the Mashed Potato Theme

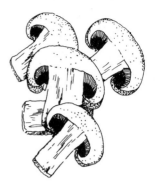

Use the basic mashed potato recipe and to it add any of the following ingredients.

Herbed potatoes

Fresh parsley	1 Tbsp (15 mL) finely chopped
Green onions	1 Tbsp (15 mL) finely chopped
Fresh chives	1 Tbsp (15 mL) finely chopped

Garlic potatoes

Garlic	2 cloves, minced
Fresh chives, optional	1 Tbsp (15 mL) finely chopped

Crowdie

Oatmeal	1/2 cup (125 mL) soaked in 1 cup (250 mL) of milk
Green onions	2 Tbsp (25 mL) finely chopped

Onion Mash

Onions	2, thinly sliced and sweated in 1 Tbsp (15 mL) butter
Cream	1/3 cup (75 mL) to replace the milk in the basic recipe
Sherry	1 Tbsp (15 mL)

Cheesed potatoes

Cheddar cheese	2/3 cup (150 mL) grated
Cayenne	1/4 tsp (1 mL)
Dry mustard	1/2 tsp (2 mL)

Spinach Spuds

Spinach	1 cup (250 mL), sweated in a little butter
Cream	1/4 cup (50 mL)
Lemon juice	1 Tbsp (15 mL)

Mushroom potatoes

Mushrooms	8, thinly sliced
Fresh tarragon	1 Tbsp (15 mL) finely chopped
Grated lemon peel	1/2 tsp (2 mL)

CHAMP

No book on potatoes would be complete without a recipe for champ. All of my Irish friends and relatives claim that champ was central to their childhoods, served almost every time they approached the table. You can peel the potatoes before cooking if you prefer, but the flavour is best if the potatoes are cooked in their skins.

Potatoes	6, scrubbed
Leeks	2
Milk	3/4 cup (175 mL)
Salt	1 tsp (5 mL)
White pepper	1/2 tsp (2 mL)
Butter	1/2 cup (125 mL) melted

1　Cut the potatoes into even-sized pieces and boil in their skins for 20 minutes or until tender.

2　Trim off the rough green sections of the leeks, retaining only the white interior leaves and the tenderest green parts. Cut off the root. With a sharp knife, slice the leeks in half lengthwise to expose the inner leaves. Hold under running water and separate the leaves to remove all the grit that clings to them. Chop the leeks coarsely.

3　While the potatoes are boiling, heat the milk to just under the boiling point and add the chopped leeks. Cook the leeks gently in the milk for 20 minutes.

4　Drain the potatoes and peel and mash them while still hot. Pour in some of the milk used to cook the leeks. Mash through and add as much milk as you need to make the potatoes the consistency you like.

5　Strain the leeks and fold into the potatoes. Season with salt and pepper.

6　Transfer the champ to a warm serving dish. Make a well in the centre and pour in the melted butter.

Serves 4–6

DUCHESS POTATOES

Hot mashed potatoes	3 cups (750 mL)
Egg yolks	3, beaten
Butter	2 Tbsp (25 mL) melted
Salt	1 tsp (5 mL)

1 While the potatoes are still hot, mix in the well-beaten egg yolks, melted butter and salt. Serve immediately.

Serves 6

DUCHESS OF CHESTER POTATOES

Same ingredients as above with the addition of:

Oil	1 Tbsp (15 mL)
Cheddar cheese	1/2 cup (125 mL) grated plus 12 thin slices

Preheat oven to 375°F (190°C).

1 Grease a shallow baking pan with the oil.

2 While the potatoes are still hot, mix in the egg yolks, butter and salt as for Duchess potatoes and also mix in the grated cheese.

3 Divide the mixture into 12 small balls. Shape the balls by hand into flat, round cakes.

4 Transfer the cakes to the greased baking pan and top each one with a slice of cheese which has been trimmed to size.

5 Bake at 375°F (190°C) for about 10 minutes or until the cheese is bubbling.

Serves 6

DAUPHINE POTATOES

This classic dish combines mashed potatoes with choux pastry. It can add a decorative touch to a special dinner party or buffet, particularly if you use a piping bag to fashion fancy shapes.

Choux pastry *	1 cup (250 mL)
Warm mashed potatoes	2 cups (500 mL)
Salt	1 tsp (5 mL)
Butter	1 Tbsp (15 mL) melted

* Recipe for choux pastry follows.

1 Make the choux pastry and set aside.

2 Preheat the oven to 425°F (220°C).

3 Combine the warm mashed potatoes, salt and choux pastry and mix well.

4 Spoon or pipe the mixture into decorative, individual servings on a greased baking sheet. The servings may be shaped into nests if you like, each nest having about 1/2 inch (1.25 cm) of the potato mixture on the bottom. The sides should be 1 1/2 – 2 inches (4 – 5 cm) high.

5 Place the potatoes on the middle rack of the 425°F (220°C) oven and immediately reduce the heat to 375°F (190°C). Bake for 20–25 minutes. Brush with melted butter before serving.

Note: This same mixture may also be shaped into balls and deep fried. Heat oil in a deep fryer to 350°F (180°C). Using two teaspoons, form the mixture into small balls. Drop the balls into the hot oil. Allow enough room for the potatoes to puff up. The balls of Dauphine mixture should be cooked at this temperature for about 3 minutes. The temperature should then be increased to 380°F (192°C), and the balls allowed to continue cooking until golden brown.

Serves 4

Choux Pastry

This recipe makes enough pastry for use in the Dauphine Potatoes.

Cold water	1/2 cup (125 mL)
Butter	1/4 cup (50 mL)
Flour	1/2 cup (125 mL) sifted
Salt	1/4 tsp (1 mL)
Eggs	2

1 In a medium-sized saucepan bring the water and butter to a boil. Remove from the heat.

2 Add the sifted flour and salt and mix well with a wooden spoon.

3 Return to a moderate heat and keep stirring until the mixture comes away from the side of the saucepan — about one minute.

4 Remove the saucepan from the heat and allow to cool a little.

5 To the warm mixture add the eggs, one at a time. Make sure the mixture is not too hot or the eggs will begin to cook and the protein will harden. Beat the first egg into the flour mixture until it is well absorbed before adding the next one. When both eggs have been completely incorporated, mix well with a wooden spoon for about 1/2 minute. The dough should be of dropping consistency.

OVEN-BAKED MASHED POTATOES

For rich, crusty, mashed potatoes try baking them in the oven. The grated cheese is optional.

Eggs	2, beaten
Cream	1/2 cup (125 mL)
Potatoes	4 medium, cooked and peeled
Butter	2 Tbsp (30 mL)
Salt	1 tsp (5 mL)
Cheddar cheese, optional	1/2 cup (125 mL) grated
Dry breadcrumbs	1/2 cup (125 mL)

Preheat oven to 375°F (190°C).

1 Combine the eggs and cream and beat together thoroughly.

2 Mash the potatoes with 1 Tbsp (15 mL) of the butter and the salt. Blend in the egg and cream mixture and add the grated cheese.

3 Grease an oven-proof dish with the remaining butter. Reserve any excess butter for use later.

4 Lightly sprinkle the greased dish with some of the breadcrumbs. Spoon in the potato mixture and spread it evenly in the dish. Top with remaining breadcrumbs. Dot with a little butter.

5 Bake at 375°F (190°C) for about 20 minutes.

Serves 4

Top: Potato and Ham Rolls (see page 85)
Bottom: Finnish Potato Pancakes (see page 153)

SNACKS AND OTHERS

Many Faces of the Potato

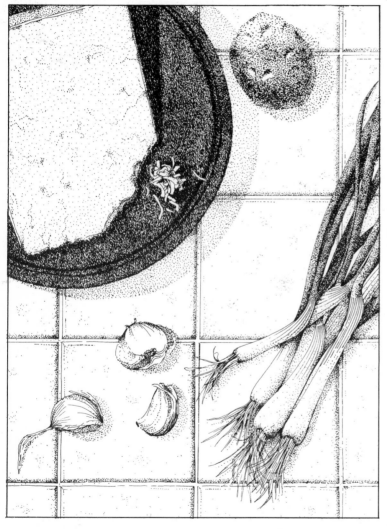

The potato is to snack foods what the lettuce is to salads — the perfect base. The French fry and the potato chip are undoubtedly two of our best-known snacks. Every corner store has its display of packaged chips, and startling new flavour combinations hit the stands every season. Potato skins are gaining popularity in restaurants and fast-food outlets. Included in this chapter are some new as well as old favourites.

Pioneer cookbooks give many unusual recipes for potatoes. Items like potato marzipan, potato fudge, sponge cakes and cookies often used mashed potatoes or potato flour as a base. A pioneer cook who had access to potatoes was fortunate indeed for necessity was the mother of invention. Luckily for us, we have other ingredients which are more appropriate than potatoes in some recipes. For this reason we chose not to include recipes which, though part of culinary history, are not likely to appeal to contemporary cooks.

On their own, potatoes are neither sweet nor savoury. Although cooking practice today has relegated potatoes mainly to the savoury food category, potatoes can absorb sugar just as easily as salt, as some of these recipes show.

Snacks

Others

WENDY'S SMOKED SALMON SHELLS

Our friend Wendy Blackwood, who runs a catering service, devised this recipe for her Christmas season canapé repertoire, and it's a particular favourite of ours. For a touch of elegance top each of these salmon shells with a dab of caviar. The potatoes may be stuffed with a variety of fillings, and another suggestion is a mixture of crab with a little cayenne and lime juice.

New potatoes	12 tiny	
Butter	1 Tbsp (15 mL)	
Spanish onion	2 Tbsp (25 mL) finely chopped	
Salt	1/2 tsp (2 mL)	
Pepper	1/4 tsp (1 mL)	
Cream cheese	2 Tbsp (25 mL)	
Smoked salmon	3 Tbsp (50 mL) chopped	

Preheat oven to 400°F (200°C).

1 Wash the potatoes well and dry with paper towels.

2 Arrange the potatoes on a lightly greased baking sheet and bake for about 35 minutes or until the potatoes are done.

3 Remove the potatoes from the oven and allow them to cool until they can be handled. Cut into halves and with a small spoon carefully scoop out most of the pulp. Reserve the pulp in a mixing bowl.

4 To the pulp add butter, onion, salt and pepper and combine well.

5 Spoon the mixture into the potato shells, filling each about three quarters full. Top each shell with a little cream cheese and finish off with the chopped smoked salmon.

Makes 24 canapés

FADGE

Fadge, a kind of savoury shortbread of Irish descent, is good for picnics and bag lunches.

Potatoes	5 medium, boiled
Flour	4 Tbsp (60 mL) sifted
Cheddar cheese	1/2 cup (125 mL) grated
Dry mustard	1/2 tsp (2 mL)
Butter	4 Tbsp (60 mL)
Salt	1 tsp (5 mL)
Pepper	1/2 tsp (2 mL)
Fresh chives	1 Tbsp (15 mL) finely chopped

1 Peel and mash the potatoes while still hot, adding 2 Tbsp (30 mL) of the butter as you mash.

2 Work in the flour and blend thoroughly. Stir in all the remaining ingredients and distribute them evenly through the mixture.

3 Place the mixture on a floured board and roll out to a thickness of 1/2 inch (1.25 cm). Cut into shapes with a cookie cutter or into triangles with a knife.

4 Melt the remaining butter and brush onto the cut-out shapes.

5 Fry in a large, greased frying pan for 3 – 5 minutes on each side; or bake on a greased baking sheet in a preheated oven at 375°F (190°C) for 30 minutes or until golden.

Makes 10 – 16 pieces, depending on size

RICK'S SPUD-FILLED PITA

I'm always looking for new ways to use up leftover mashed potatoes, and this is about as easy as you can get. If you prefer to serve the pita cold, just line each pita with lettuce leaves and spoon in the filling.

Anchovy fillets	1 can, 2-oz (57-g)
Mashed potatoes	2 cups (500 mL)
Red onion	1 small, peeled and finely chopped
Black olives	6 – 8, chopped
Canned tuna	2 Tbsp (25 mL) drained and flaked
Plain yoghurt	2 Tbsp (25 mL)
Pepper	1/4 tsp (1 mL)
Pita bread	4, about 5 1/2 inches (14 cm) diameter

Preheat oven to 350°F (180°C).

1 Chop the anchovy fillets and in a large mixing bowl combine all the ingredients except the pita. Mix thoroughly.

2 Cut off a slice from the edge of each pita to open a pocket.

3 Spoon the filling into the pocket and heat in the oven for 10 – 15 minutes or until the filling has warmed through.

Serves 4

CURRIED CABBAGE ROLLS

Cabbage leaves make a delicious wrapping for many fillings, and this curried filling is particularly easy to make. These rolls can be made ahead of time and frozen, making them an ideal and interesting addition to party fare.

Large cabbage leaves	12
Ghee or clarified butter*	1 Tbsp (15 mL)
Onion	1 small, peeled and finely chopped
Ground turmeric	1/2 tsp (2 mL)
Chili powder	1/2 tsp (2 mL)
Ground cumin	1/2 tsp (2 mL)
Mashed potatoes	3 cups (750 mL)
Garlic	1 clove, minced
Salt	1/2 tsp (2 mL)
Pepper	1/4 tsp (1 mL)
Fresh coriander	1 tsp (5 mL) finely chopped
Fresh parsley	2 tsp (10 mL) finely chopped
Oil	3 Tbsp (50 mL)

* Oil may be substituted for ghee

1 Soften the cabbage leaves by parboiling them for 5 minutes. Cut out the hard vein in the centre of each leaf.

2 In a large frying pan melt the ghee and add the chopped onions, turmeric, chili powder and cumin and fry gently for about 1 minute.

3 In a large mixing bowl combine the mashed potatoes, minced garlic, salt, pepper, coriander and parsley with the onions, spices and ghee from the frying pan. Mix together thoroughly.

4 Spread the cabbage leaves on a flat surface. Divide the curried potato mixture into 12 portions and place 1 portion on each leaf. Roll up into neat parcels and tie with thread.

5 Heat the oil and fry the cabbage rolls over medium heat until browned on each side. Drain on paper towels. Remove the thread and serve.

Makes 12 cabbage rolls

CURRIED POTATO SNACKS

Serve these with mango chutney or herbed yoghurt dip. You may choose to replace the turmeric, cumin and chili with a tsp (5 mL) of prepared curry powder.

Chili powder	1/4 tsp (1 mL)
Ground cumin	1/4 tsp (1 mL)
Ground turmeric	1/4 tsp (1 mL)
Salt	1/2 tsp (2 mL)
Mashed potatoes	3 cups (750 mL)
Onion	1, peeled and finely chopped
Garlic	1 clove, minced
Fresh coriander, optional	1 tsp (5 mL) finely chopped
Oil	3 Tbsp (50 mL)

1 Mix together the first 4 ingredients and put them in a large bowl. Mix in all the remaining ingredients except the oil and blend thoroughly by hand or with a fork.

2 Shape into small cakes about 1 inch (2.5 cm) across and 1/2 inch (1.25 cm) thick.

3 Heat the oil in a large frying pan and fry the potato cakes until crisp on both sides.

Makes about 12 snacks

PERUNAPIIRAKKAA — POTATO PIES

Rick first tasted these potato pies in Helsinki, in the open-air market beside the harbour, where they sell many varieties of these flat, oval-shaped, chewy pies made from rye flour and filled with savoury potato or rice.

You can flavour the potato filling to suit your own taste by adding herbs such as dill or chives, grated cheese or something more tangy, such as anchovies, sliced olives or chilies.

Rye crust (recipe follows)	16 oz (450 g)
Whipped potatoes	4 cups (1 L)
Cheddar cheese	1 cup (250 mL) grated
Fresh dill	3 Tbsp (50 mL) chopped
Milk	1/4 cup (50 mL)
Butter	2 Tbsp (25 mL) melted
Salt	1/2 tsp (2 mL)
Pepper	1/2 tsp (2 mL)

Rye crust

Rye flour	2 cups (500 mL) sifted
All-purpose white flour	1 cup (250 mL) sifted
Salt	1/2 tsp (2 mL)
Butter	3 Tbsp (50 mL)
Water	1 cup (250 mL)

1 To make the crust sift the flour and salt together in a mixing bowl.

2 With a fork cut in the butter until the fat is broken into small pieces. Finish the rubbing-in process with your fingertips. Rub the fat into the flour until the mixture resembles the texture of breadcrumbs. Make a well in the centre.

3 Into the well add some of the water and gradually draw the mixture into the liquid, using a fork or your fingers. Add more water as necessary until the mixture comes away from the sides of the bowl and holds together. Round the dough into a ball and rest it in the refrigerator for 30 minutes.

4 On a floured surface, roll out the dough 1/8 inch (3 mm) thick and cut into a dozen 6-inch (15-cm) circles. Stack and rest them in the refrigerator while you make the filling.

5 Preheat the oven to 425°F (220°C).

6 To make the filling combine all the ingredients in a large mixing bowl. Blend with an electric mixer until the mixture is finely whipped.

7 Spoon about 3 Tbsp (50 mL) of the filling onto each circle of pastry. Spread it over the dough, leaving a space around the edge. Take the opposite sides of the pastry circle and fold in towards the centre. Do not overlap the pastry; leave a 1-inch (2.5-cm) space down the middle to expose the filling. Turn up and pinch the unfolded edges of the pastry to form an oval. Crimp the edges with your fingers.

8 Bake the perunapiirakka on a greased baking sheet for 20 to 30 minutes or until the pastry is browned. To make the crust chewy, baste the pies with a mixture of hot milk and melted butter while they are baking. For this number of pies, heat 1/2 cup (125 mL) milk and 2 Tbsp (25 mL) butter. Baste twice during baking and once when the pies have been removed from the oven.

9 Cover the pies with a clean towel or foil to keep the crust chewy. Serve hot or cold.

Makes 12 pies

DEEP-FRIED POTATO SCALLOPS

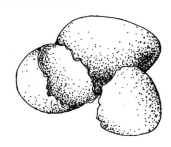

These potato scallops were an essential part of my youth and the ritual of the Saturday movie matinee. With the ten cents change left over from the price of admission (this was eons ago, before inflation had stripped ten cents of all meaning), we bought a fistful of freshly fried scallops. They were *our* neighbourhood's answer to patate frites.

Egg	1, beaten
Milk	1 cup (250 mL)
Flour	1 cup (250 mL) sifted *
Salt	1/2 tsp (2 mL)
Potatoes	4 large, peeled
Oil	for deep frying

*Plus a little extra to dust the potato slices.

1 In a mixing bowl combine the beaten egg and the milk and mix well. Sift in the flour and salt. Stir to combine the ingredients and to remove any lumps, but do not overmix or beat. Rest the batter in the refrigerator for 1/2 an hour.

2 Cut the potatoes into slices about 1/4 inch (6 mm) thick. Soak them in cold water for 5 minutes. Drain and dry well.

3 Heat the oil to 375°F (190°C) for deep frying.

4 Dust each potato slice with flour, then coat each slice thoroughly with the batter and drop into the hot oil. Cook only a few at a time. Each batch will take about 10 minutes. Keep the scallops warm until all of the scallops are deep fried. Serve hot, sprinkled with extra salt.

Makes about 24 scallops

OVEN-BAKED CHIPS

There are many ways to cut these chips — in rounds, sticks or wedges. You can slice them thinly in a food processor or make chunky ones by hand. Naturally, the thicker the slice, the longer they will need to stay in the oven. If they're about 1/2 inch (1.25 cm) thick, for example, you'll need to bake them approximately 20 minutes on each side. I prefer to leave the skins on.

Garlic, optional	2 cloves, crushed
Oil	1/3 cup (75 mL)
Potatoes	6 large
Salt	1 tsp (5 mL)

Preheat oven to 375°F (190°C).

1 Let the crushed garlic stand in the oil while you prepare the potatoes.

2 Scrub the potatoes well and slice in whatever manner you prefer. Cover the cut potatoes with cold water and allow to stand for 5 minutes. Drain and dry the potatoes with a clean towel or paper towel.

3 Put the potatoes in a bowl and pour the oil over them. Toss to coat each slice. Sprinkle with salt and turn the slices over to distribute the salt evenly.

4 Arrange the potatoes on a non-stick baking sheet. Do not overlap the slices.

5 Bake at 375°F (190°C) for approximately 20 minutes on each side, depending on the thickness. Thin chips cut in a food processor will not need to be turned.

Serves 4

POTATO CHEESE PUFFS

You can add any of your favourite herbs or seasonings to this mixture; the combination listed here is just right for my family's taste. For a little extra texture, coat the balls in egg-wash and breadcrumbs before baking.

Potatoes	5 large, boiled, peeled and mashed
Eggs	2, beaten
Flour	3 Tbsp (50 mL)
Cheddar cheese	1 cup (250 mL) grated
Fresh parsley	2 Tbsp (25 mL) finely chopped
Dried mixed herbs (oregano, basil, thyme, parsley)	1 tsp (5 mL) finely ground
Salt	1 tsp (5 mL)
Pepper	1/2 tsp (2 mL)
Oil	1 Tbsp (15 mL)

Preheat oven to 375°F (190°C).

1 Combine all the ingredients except the oil and mix thoroughly. Shape the mixture by hand into small balls about 1 inch (2.5 cm) in diameter.

2 Grease a baking sheet with the oil and place the balls on the sheet. Bake at 375°F (190°C) for approximately 25 minutes or until browned.

Makes about 16 balls

BAKED POTATO SKINS

Potato skins can be served with spiced or herbed sour cream or your own favourite dip.

Potatoes	12 small
Butter	1/2 cup (125 mL) melted

Preheat oven to 400°F (200°C).

1 Scrub the potatoes and wipe them dry. Place them on a baking sheet and bake at 400°F (200°C) until done — about 45 minutes, depending on the size.

2 Remove the potatoes from the oven and cut into halves. Spoon out the pulp into a mixing bowl, but leave a little of the pulp attached to the skin so that the shells will retain their shape. Set the pulp aside for another use (for example, see the recipe for Irish Apple-Potato Pie).

3 Reduce the oven temperature to 375°F (190°C). Brush the outsides of the empty skins with a little melted butter. Invert the skins and arrange them skin side up on a baking sheet.

4 Return to the oven for 10 – 15 minutes or until they have reached the crispness you like.

Makes 24 skins

DEEP-FRIED POTATO SKINS

Take 12 small potatoes and prepare them according to the previous recipe up to and including Step 2. Heat oil for deep frying to about 375°F (190°C). Fry until crisp. Drain well.

Peelings from scrubbed potatoes may also be deep fried. Carefully peel large potatoes, keeping the strips of skin intact. Soak the peelings in cold water for about 5 minutes. Drain and dry thoroughly, then either deep fry or oven bake (brush them with a little butter if you bake them) until crisp. Sprinkle with salt.

POTATO DUMPLINGS

These dumplings are a fine addition to Irish stew, curries or hearty soups. They can also be steamed or pan fried and sprinkled with chopped herbs or cheese and served separately.

Mashed potatoes	2 cups (500 mL)
All-purpose or potato flour	3 Tbsp (50 mL)
Oil	2 Tbsp (25 mL)
Garlic	1 clove, minced
Eggs	2, beaten
Milk	2 Tbsp (25 mL)
Fresh mixed herbs (e.g. parsley, chives, basil)	2 Tbsp (25 mL) finely chopped
Salt	1/2 tsp (2 mL)

1 Combine all the ingredients and knead gently by hand to incorporate into a firm mixture. Add extra milk if the texture seems dry or extra flour if it's too wet.

2 Scoop out a spoonful of the mixture and shape into a small ball. Continue until all of the mixture is used up.

3 Drop the balls into simmering water or add them to hot soups or stews. Allow the dumplings to simmer, covered with a lid, for approximately 5 minutes before serving.

Makes 8 – 10 dumplings, depending on the size

POTATO-APPLE DUMPLINGS

Next time you roast pork, try these dumplings as a side dish. They're wonderful laced with pork gravy.

Cooking apple	1, peeled and cored
Lemon juice	1/2 tsp (2 mL)
Mashed potatoes	2 cups (500 mL)
All-purpose or potato flour	2 Tbsp (25 mL)
Fresh dill	2 tsp (10 mL) finely chopped
Salt	1/4 tsp (1 mL)
Eggs	2, beaten
Dry breadcrumbs	1 cup (250 mL)
Butter	1 Tbsp (15 mL)

1 Grate the apple and sprinkle with a little lemon juice to prevent browning. Mix in the potatoes, flour, dill, salt and one beaten egg. Mix well and shape by hand into 1-inch (2.5-cm) dumplings. Flatten the dumplings with the back of a knife.

2 Beat the remaining egg with a little water to make an egg-wash. Spread the breadcrumbs on a dinner plate to coat the dumplings.

3 Dip the dumplings first in the egg-wash, coating thoroughly, and then in the breadcrumbs. Coat each dumpling twice to give a firm seal. Set them on a platter and refrigerate for 20 minutes before baking.

4 Preheat oven to 350°F (180°C). Arrange the dumplings on a well-buttered baking sheet and bake for 20 – 25 minutes or until golden.

Serves 4

PLUM DUMPLINGS

These sweet dumplings can be very filling, so they're best served after a light meal of soup or salad. When plums are in season, make the whole dumplings, but when they're not available, you can make just the sweet dough for a satisfying and unusual after-dinner snack. To do this cook small portions of the dough in boiling water and roll them in breadcrumbs, sugar, cinnamon and crushed walnuts.

Mashed potatoes	3 1/2 cups (875 mL)
Egg	1, beaten
Flour	1 cup (250 mL) sifted
Sugar	1/2 cup (125 mL)
Ground cinnamon	2 tsp (10 mL)
Plums	6
Butter	2 Tbsp (25 mL)
Dry breadcrumbs	1 cup (250 mL)

1 In a mixing bowl combine the mashed potatoes, egg and flour to form a dough.

2 In another bowl combine the sugar and cinnamon.

3 Wash the plums and carefully cut out the seeds. Into each cavity spoon a little of the sugar and cinnamon mixture, reserving some to sprinkle on the cooked dumplings.

4 Divide the dough into six portions. Roll out one portion of dough and place a plum in the centre. Draw the dough up around the plum and press the pastry together to seal completely. If the pastry does not stick, wet your fingers and lightly moisten the dough wherever it needs to be sealed. Lightly press the dough around the plum with slightly wet hands. Repeat for each plum.

5 Bring a large pot of water to a boil. Carefully drop the dumplings, a few at a time, into the boiling water. Keep the water boiling gently as the dumplings cook — about 10 minutes. Remove from the water with a slotted spoon and drain well.

6 In a frying pan melt the butter, then add the breadcrumbs and brown them. Place the cooked dumplings in the breadcrumbs and roll them gently to coat completely. Remove the dumplings to a platter and sprinkle them with the remaining sugar and cinnamon mixture. Serve hot.

Makes 6 dumplings

JOHNNY CAKES

My father called these "girdle" scones. He enjoyed playing about with language almost as much as he liked these griddle scones.

Potatoes	4 medium, cooked and mashed
Egg	1, beaten
Flour	1 cup (250 mL)
Baking powder	1 tsp (5 mL)
Pepper	1/4 tsp (1 mL)
Fresh chives	1 Tbsp (15 mL) finely chopped
Butter	3 Tbsp (50 mL) melted

1 In a mixing bowl beat together the potatoes and egg with a wooden spoon.

2 Sift the dry ingredients and add the chopped chives. Knead quickly into a ball.

3 Make a hole in the centre of the mixture and pour in 2 Tbsp (25 mL) of the melted butter. Knead again until the butter is absorbed.

4 Roll out the mixture onto a floured board until it's about 1/2 inch (1.25 cm) thick. Cut into 2-inch (5-cm) circles.

5 With the remaining butter grease a heavy frying pan or the top of a griddle. If you use a frying pan, drain off the excess butter. Reserve the extra in case you need it when you fry the Johnny cakes.

6 Fry the cakes in several batches, depending on the size of your griddle or pan. Fry until golden; this should take about 8 minutes on each side. The scones may cook faster on a griddle.

7 If you prefer, the scones may be baked in an oven preheated to 400°F (200°C) for 12 to 15 minutes or until they are golden.

Makes approximately 12 Johnny cakes

Note: For an interesting variation try adding the following season-ing — 1 tsp (5 mL) each of dry mustard and finely chopped fresh dill and a pinch of cayenne.

IRISH APPLE-POTATO PIE

This Irish recipe was devised, no doubt, out of necessity. When potatoes are abundant, you find all kinds of things to make with them.

Potatoes	4 medium, peeled and boiled
Butter	2 Tbsp (30 mL)
Ground cinnamon	1/8 tsp (0.5 mL)
Ground ginger	1/8 tsp (0.5 mL)
Brown sugar	2 Tbsp (25 mL)
Flour	4 Tbsp (60 mL)
Cooking apples	4, peeled and cored

Preheat oven to 375°F (190°C).

1 While the potatoes are still hot, put them into a large mixing bowl and mash them with 1 Tbsp (15 mL) of the butter, cinnamon, ginger and half of the sugar.

2 Incorporate the flour, blending well. Divide the mixture into 2 parts, one slightly larger than the other.

3 Roll or shape each into a flat circle and trim the edges. Transfer the larger circle onto a well-greased baking sheet.

4 Slice the apples and arrange the slices in a mound in the centre of the larger circle. Sprinkle the apples with half of the remaining sugar.

5 Brush the edge of the larger circle with water and cover the apples with the smaller circle of dough. Fold the bottom edge up and crimp the edges together to seal.

6 Cut an X in the top of the pie as a vent for the steam. Bake at 375°F (190°C) for 40 minutes.

7 Remove from the oven, brush with a little butter and sprinkle with the remaining sugar. Put the remaining butter and, if you wish, an extra sprinkle of sugar into the vent. Serve hot.

Serves 4 – 6

LATKES

Chicken soup, knishes and latkes (potato pancakes) are important components of Jewish cuisine. Every mother has her own recipe and secret ingredients; some use matzoh meal instead of flour to make latkes. You'll find that the latkes are crisper and firmer if the batter is made ahead of time and left to rest in the refrigerator for an hour or so.

Potatoes	4 raw, grated
Onion	1, peeled and grated
Sour cream	1 Tbsp (15 mL)
Salt	1/2 tsp (2 mL)
Pepper	1/2 tsp (2 mL)
Eggs	2, beaten
Flour	2 Tbsp (25 mL)
Butter	2 Tbsp (25 mL)
Oil	1 Tbsp (15 mL)

1 Squeeze out the liquid from the grated potatoes and grated onions and combine in a large mixing bowl. Add the sour cream and salt and pepper. Beat in the eggs, then gradually add the flour and incorporate it well. Set aside in the refrigerator for an hour or so. The mixture can be made the night before and cooked the next morning for breakfast.

2 Heat the butter and oil in a large frying pan. Spoon in the batter, leaving space for each latke to spread. Fry on both sides until brown and crisp.

3 Place on paper towels to drain off the excess fat. Keep the latkes warm until all the batter has been cooked.

Makes about 10 3-inch (7.5-cm) latkes

FISH STUFFING

Fish may be cooked with or without stuffing, but remember to allow an extra 10 minutes to the cooking time for a stuffed fish. This delicious stuffing absorbs the juices of the fish as it cooks, and this quantity will do for a large round fish such as salmon.

Once the fish is scaled and gutted, wash it thoroughly and rub out the belly cavity with a little salt and then lemon juice. You may remove the head and tail if you wish. Fill the cavity with the stuffing and secure it with small skewers or stitch the cavity closed with a needle and strong thread. The fish may be poached, baked or barbecued. A 6-lb (2.7-kg) stuffed salmon will cook in approximately 40 minutes.

Butter	1 Tbsp (15 mL)
Onion	1 medium, peeled and finely chopped
Potatoes	2 medium, cooked and mashed
Egg	1 yolk, beaten
Garlic	1 clove, minced
Cream	2 Tbsp (25 mL)
Grated lemon peel*	from 1/2 a lemon
Fresh parsley or dill	1 Tbsp (15 mL) finely chopped
Salt	1/4 tsp (1 mL)
White pepper	1/4 tsp (1 mL)

*With a fine grater remove just the yellow surface of the skin of a lemon. This will give you a fresh, concentrated lemon flavour from the oils and fibre on the surface, without the bitterness of the white membrane underneath.

1 In a small saucepan melt the butter and fry the chopped onions until soft — about 5 minutes.

2 Combine all the ingredients in a large bowl and mix thoroughly.

3 Prepare the fish and spoon the stuffing into the cavity. Close the cavity with toothpicks, skewers or stitch it with strong thread.

POULTRY STUFFING

This quantity is enough for a small turkey or goose.

Lemon	1
Dry bread	2 slices
Celery	2 small stalks including leaves
Potatoes	4 large, cooked and mashed
Onion	1, peeled and finely chopped
Eggs	2, beaten
Garlic	1 clove, minced
Dried sage	1 tsp (5 mL)
Salt	1 tsp (5 mL)
Sherry	1 Tbsp (15 mL)

1 Squeeze the juice from the lemon and set aside the lemon skin.

2 Rub the cavity of the bird with the outside of the lemon skin, then discard the skin.

3 In a large mixing bowl break up the dry bread by pulling it into small pieces with your fingers. Finely chop the celery stalks and leaves and add with all remaining ingredients to the bowl. Mix thoroughly.

4 Stuff the bird and truss it with either skewers or string. Baking time will depend on the size of the bird.

ILMI'S POTATO BREAD

This is a dark, substantial bread similar to the potato bread or *perunaleipa* that Rick's grandmother Ilmi Kallio used to make. Every time we make it, the odour of the yeast and rye flour transports Rick back to her kitchen and the memory of that first piece of chewy crust slathered in butter. We've modified the recipe, replacing some of the rye flour with white flour. For the dill you may substitute chives or another herb to suit your taste, but the hint of dill is particularly evocative of things Finnish: it goes well with *kalamojakka* (the recipe can be found in the section on soups).

Potatoes	8 large
Potato water	1 1/2 cups (375 mL), tepid
Molasses or corn syrup or honey	2 Tbsp (25 mL)
Active dry yeast	2 Tbsp (25 mL) or 2 packets
Rye flour	6 cups (1.5 L)
White, all-purpose flour	4 cups (1 L)
Salt	1 Tbsp (15 mL)
Fresh dill	1/2 cup (125 mL) finely chopped
Oil	1/4 cup (50 mL)

Note: Instead of adding all the ingredients to the activated yeast and potato water mixture, we will use the sponge method. The sponge, a mixture of potato water, yeast and about one-third of the flour will be set aside to rise for about 60 minutes while the rest of the ingredients are mixed and prepared for blending with the sponge. This method allows for an extra working of the yeast because rye flour does not rise as much as white flour.

1   Boil the potatoes without adding salt. When draining the potatoes, save 1 1/2 cups (375 mL) of the potato water. Mash and whip the potatoes with an electric mixer, but do not add any milk or butter. Measure out 4 cups (1 L) of mashed potatoes, cover and set aside to cool.

2   To make the sponge, allow the potato water to cool to about 95°F (35°C). If you have no thermometer, test the water on your wrist — it should feel warm but not hot. Add a drop of the molasses (or corn syrup or honey). Sprinkle the dry yeast into the water, mix lightly and let stand for about 10 minutes until the yeast becomes activated and forms a froth on top of the water.

3   Transfer the yeast mixture to a mixing bowl. Gradually add 2 cups (500 mL) of the rye flour and 1 cup (250 mL) of the white flour. Beat together the flour and the mixture with a whisk or a wooden spoon until it becomes a sticky mass.

4 Cover the bowl containing the sponge with a damp cloth and put it in a warm place to allow the sponge to rise for approximately 60 minutes.

5 Place the cooled mashed potatoes in another bowl and with a wooden spoon thoroughly mix in 1 Tbsp (15 mL) salt, 2 Tbsp (25 mL) molasses (or corn syrup or honey) and the chopped dill. Then gradually add, 1/4 cup (50 mL) at a time, the rye and white flour, reserving about 1 cup (250 mL) to be added when the dough is kneaded.

6 Mix the flour thoroughly with the other ingredients. It's best to use both hands to rub and combine the mixture into a ball.

7 When the sponge has risen, combine the ball of dough with the sponge. You might need to add a little of the reserved flour while mixing.

8 Knead the dough mixture on a floured surface for approximately 30 minutes. Add just enough flour while kneading to keep the dough from sticking to the surface. Form the dough into a ball.

9 Oil a mixing bowl. Put the ball of dough into the bowl and turn the dough until it's entirely covered with a thin film of oil. This prevents it from drying out while it is rising. Cover the bowl with a damp cloth and put it in a warm spot. Let the dough rise for one hour. Don't worry if the dough does not rise dramatically — the rye flour and the addition of mashed potato cuts down a little on the rising.

10 After the dough has risen, punch it down and transfer it to the floured surface. Knead the dough again for approximately 30 minutes.

11 Divide the dough in half and shape each half into a round loaf.

12 Spread aluminum foil on a baking tray and coat the foil with a thin film of oil. Place the loaves of dough on the foil, cover with a damp cloth and let them rise again for about 30 minutes.

13 While the dough is rising preheat the oven to 375°F (190°C).

14 Bake the bread for 50–60 minutes.

15 Remove the bread from the oven and let sit for 20 minutes before slicing.

Makes 2 loaves

POTATO-ALMOND CAKE

Serve this cake plain or with a creamy frosting, topped with roasted slivered almonds.

Potato flour	1 cup sifted
Baking powder	1 tsp (5 mL)
Salt	1/4 tsp (1 mL)
Eggs	3, separated
Honey	1/3 cup (75 mL)
Sour cream	1/2 cup (125 mL)
Slivered almonds	1/3 cup (75 mL)

Preheat oven to 350°F (180°C).

1 Sift together the potato flour, baking powder and salt.

2 Beat the egg yolks until thick. Blend in the honey, sour cream and slivered almonds.

3 In a separate bowl, beat the egg whites until stiff. Gently fold the whites into the yolks, a little at a time, alternating with the sifted potato flour.

4 Bake in a greased 9-inch (2.5-L) cake tin for 40 minutes. Do not open the oven door during the first 20 minutes of baking.

5 When the cake is done turn it out onto a wire rack to cool.

Serves 6

FINNISH POTATO PANCAKES

Pancakes have a special virtue: they can be made ahead of time and warmed in the oven just before serving. This recipe makes a rich, thick pancake that crisps at the edges as it fries.

Cream	2 Tbsp (25 mL)
Sour cream	2 Tbsp (25 mL)
Eggs	2, beaten
Butter	2 Tbsp (25 mL)
Potato flour	3 Tbsp (50 mL)
Salt	1/2 tsp (2 mL)
Potatoes	4 large, peeled and grated
Cooked ham	1/2 cup (125 mL) finely chopped
Fresh chives	1 Tbsp (15 mL) freshly chopped

1 Combine the cream, sour cream and well-beaten eggs in a mixing bowl.

2 Melt the butter in a frying pan over medium heat and distribute the butter well over the surface. Remove the pan from the heat and allow to cool a little. Leaving just enough butter to coat the pan, pour off any excess into the egg mixture and blend through.

3 Mix the flour and salt into the egg mixture and beat well by hand to incorporate the flour thoroughly.

4 Press any liquid out of the grated potatoes and pat dry with paper towels.

5 Add the potatoes, ham and chives to the batter and stir through. Allow the mixture to rest in the refrigerator for 1/2 hour.

6 Reheat the frying pan. Drop a small amount of the batter into the pan to test the temperature. If the edges become firm immediately, the pan is ready.

7 Stir the mixture and, using a large spoon, drop the mixture into the pan. Carefully distribute the pieces of ham and potato over the surface of each pancake. Fry gently until firm and slightly crisp on each side.

Makes about 12 3-inch (7.5-cm) pancakes

POTATO TOPPING

Seasoned mashed potatoes can be used as a topping or upper crust for many different casseroles, cottage pies or fish bakes. Not only does the potato extend the other ingredients in the dish to provide more servings, the topping adds a smooth, creamy contrast in texture.

The potatoes may be spooned onto the casserole and distributed evenly across the top with the back of a spoon or fork. If you have a piping bag, you can produce a very decorative topping.

Mashed potatoes	3 cups (750 mL)
Butter	1 Tbsp (15 mL)
Onion	1 medium, peeled and grated
Salt	1 tsp (5 mL)
Sour cream, optional	1 Tbsp (15 mL)
Fresh parsley, optional	1 Tbsp (15 mL) finely chopped
Cayenne, optional	1/4 tsp (1 mL)

1 Combine all the ingredients and mix together thoroughly.

2 Spread the mixture on top of the casserole and bake in a moderate oven for about 20 minutes or until golden.

Makes enough to cover a 9-inch (2.5-L) casserole

CHRISTMAS CANDIES

These candies may be made with chunky peanut butter for a crunchy texture.

Mashed potatoes	2 cups (500 mL)
Vanilla extract	1 tsp (5 mL)
Icing sugar	1 1/2 cups (375 mL)
Peanut butter	1/2 cup (125 mL)
Flaked almonds	2 Tbsp (25 mL), lightly roasted

1 Combine all the ingredients except the flaked almonds. Knead together by hand to thoroughly work in the sugar.

2 Press onto a cookie sheet and trim the edges. Sprinkle with flaked almonds and press the almonds into the top of the mixture. Cut into small squares but leave them on the cookie sheet.

3 Refrigerate for about 5 hours, until the candies are firm. Remove from the cookie sheet and serve.

Makes about 30 squares.

Index

Kitchen Metrics

For cooking and baking convenience, the Metric Commission of Canada suggests the following for adapting to metric measurement. The table gives approximate rather than exact conversions.

SPOONS

1/4 tsp	1 mL
1/2 tsp	2 mL
1 tsp	5 mL
1 Tbsp	15 mL
2 Tbsp	25 mL *
3 Tbsp	50 mL

CUPS

1/4 cup	50 mL
1/3 cup	75 mL
1/2 cup	125 mL
2/3 cup	150 mL
3/4 cup	175 mL
1 cup	250 mL

OVEN TEMPERATURE

200°F	100°C	350°F	180°C
225°F	110°C	375°F	190°C
250°F	120°C	400°F	200°C
275°F	140°C	425°F	220°C
300°F	150°C	450°F	230°C
325°F	160°C	475°F	240°C

*In some recipes you will note that the metric equivalent of 2 Tbsp is shown as 30 mL instead of 25 mL. This occurs when the ingredient is used in two parts, 1 Tbsp (15 mL) at a time.